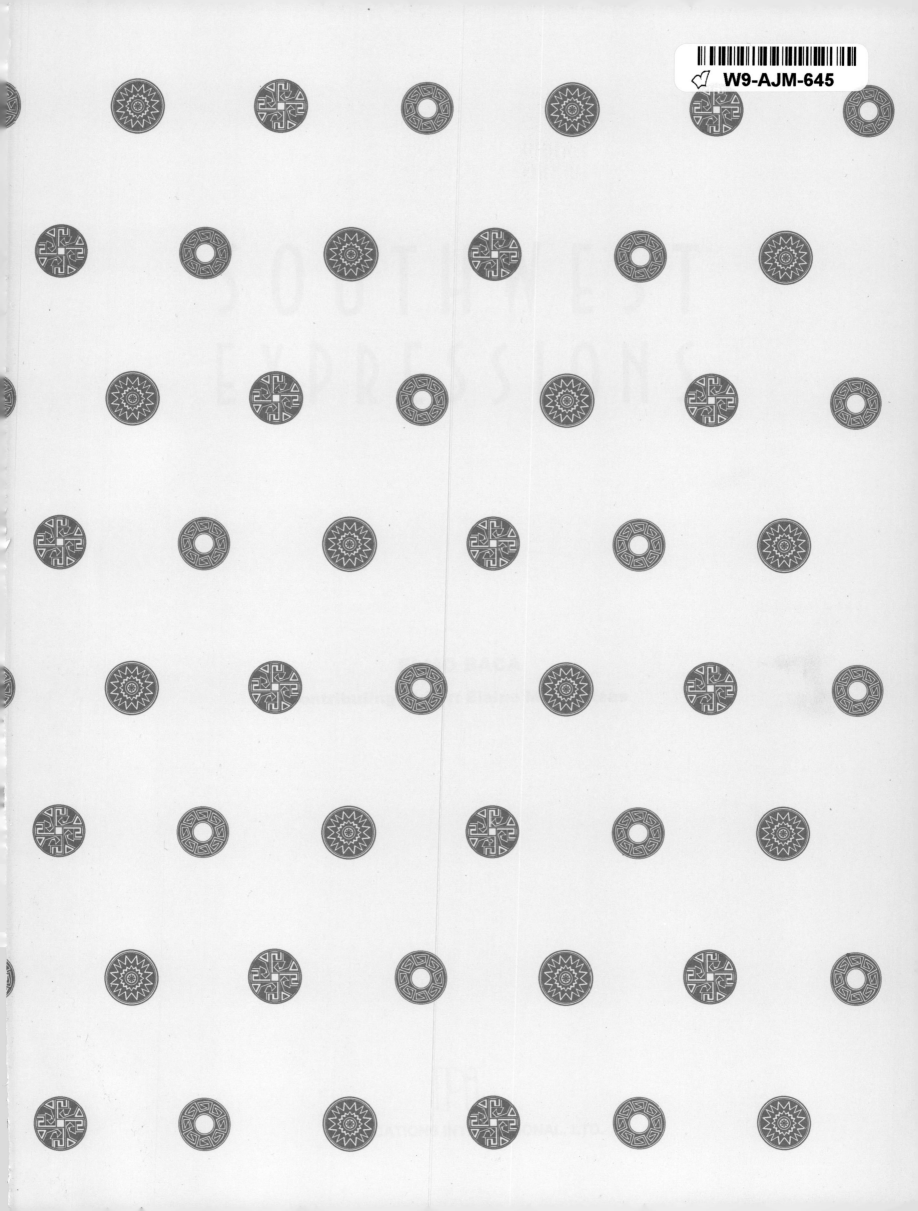

Elmo Baca is a historic preservation-ist and writer, who has a degree in architecture from Yale University. He is the executive director of the Gallup Downtown Development Group and is a frequent contributor to *New Mexico Magazine.*

Elaine Markoutsas, a nationally syn-dicated design columnist, is a field editor for *Better Homes & Gardens* and a contributor to *HG, Home,* and *1001 Home Ideas.* She was formerly the director of home furnishings for the Merchandise Mart in Chicago.

Special acknowledgment to Carla Breeze, who has authored two publications entitled *Pueblo Deco.*

Architects and Designers Acknowledgements:
Anderson, Mason & Dale, Denver, CO; Thomas J. Ashe Contractor, Inc., Placitas, NM; The Aspen Group, Aspen, CO; Paula Berg Design Associates, Scottsdale, AZ; Mark Butler, Butler Construction, Tucson, AZ; Will Bruder Studio, New River, AZ; Ed Chamberlin Architects, P.C., Grand Junction, CO; Adolf deRoy Mark & Associates, Carefree, AZ, and Philadelphia, PA; Designers Circle Ltd., Los Angeles, CA; Design West, Aspen, CO; Ford, Powell & Carson Inc., San Antonio, TX; W. A. Foster Co., Chicago, IL; John Grayble; San Antonio, TX; Berent Groth, Albuquerque, NM; Inter Plan Design Group, Scottsdale, AZ; Carlos Jimenez Design Studio, Houston, TX; Kailer-Grant & Associates, Santa Fe, NM; Robert Kahler, Austin, TX; Carla Kalwaitis Designs, Palm Springs, CA; Kitchell Interior Design Associates, Scottsdale, AZ; Knoell & Quidort Architects, Phoenix, AZ; The Kohler Co., Kohler, WI; Lake/Flato Architects, San Antonio, TX; Jackie Mallory Design Studio, Albuquerque, NM; L. Mehren Limited Additions, Scottsdale, AZ; Heather McKinney Architects, Austin, TX; McHugh Lloyd Tryk, Santa Fe, NM; Mongerson Wunderlich, Chicago, IL; National Upholstering Co., Oakland, CA; The Naturalist Furniture Co., Provo, UT; Robert L. Nevins, Phoenix, AZ; Pearson & Co., Scottsdale, AZ; Peterson Architects, Menlo Park, CA; Bart Prince Architect, Albuquerque, NM; Rob Wellington Quigley Architect, San Diego, CA; Reed Bros., Sebastopol, CA; Ronchetti Design Group, Rancho Santa Fe, CA; Charles Schiffner Architects, Ltd., Phoenix, AZ; Alexander Seidel & Associates, San Francisco, CA; Southwest Doors, Tucson, AZ; Spears Architects, Santa Fe, NM; Lawrence Speck, Austin, TX; William Tull, Carefree, AZ; Westwork Architects, Albuquerque, NM; Wilson & Associates Interior Architectural Design, Dallas, TX; Barbara Windum, Santa Fe, NM.

Photo Credits

Cover photos: Deck: Kirk Gittings Photography/ McHugh Lloyd Tryk, Architects; Pot & Basket: **Jerry Jacka**; Skull: **Dick Kaplan/Southwest Sampler.**

Back cover: Carla Breeze: bottom center & bottom right; **Kirk Gittings/Syntax:** top right; **John Olsen:** center; **Michael Skott:** top center & center right; **Dick Kaplan/Southwest Sampler:** top left; **Charles S. White:** center left & bottom left.

KEY
Numbers indicate pages.

C—Center	R—Right	L—Left
T—Top	TR—Top Right	TL—Top Left
B—Bottom	BR—Bottom Right	BL—Bottom Left

Peter Aaron/Esto Photographics: 13, 14, 20T, 29-30, 33, 86L, 156-157, 158-159, 222-223; **Elmo Baca:** 11R, 27C, 51T, 55BL, 55BL&BR, 67C, 74, 75R&C, 83, 87, 94T&R, 108, 109T, 113, 114T&L, 117TR,

124B, 126, 127, 146R, 155B; **Mark Boisclair:** 203T, 208, 209, 210-211, 211; **Bob Brazell:** 52, 53; **Carla Breeze:** 167, 206, 207R, 220-221, 242, 243T&R, 254T, 255; **Ken Bresset:** 105B; **Arthur Coleman:** 66, 69, 70-71, 84-85, 88-89; **Lisl Dennis/McHugh-Lloyd-Tryk, Architects:** 237; **Adolf DeRoy-Mark & Associates, Architects:** 63T, 149R, 163, 236R; **W.A. Foster Co.:** 174C; **Ford, Powell & Carson, Inc.:** 61, 194, 195T, 231C, 250-251; **FPG International:** David M. Boody: 199B; Jeri Gleiter: 192B; Ed Taylor: 196R; **Eduardo Fuss:** 7T, 8T, 16L, 19R, 24L&R, 25, 27B, 28, 31B&C, 36B, 38, 39T&R, 40, 43, 45, 47L, 48T, 55T, 84, 90B, 93R, 94L, 98B, 133T&B, 134B, 141R, 142, 146T, 149B, 154, 155L, 169BL, 203C&B, 204T&B, 205, 231B, 248; **Eduardo Fuss/Dewey Galleries, LTD:** 19R, 27B, 71, 141T, 145L, 215, 217L, 232; **John J. Gillan:** 150, 151; **Kirk Gittings/Syntax:** 20B, 21, 26, 34, 41-42, 56B, 57, 136, 144, 152L&B, 153, 216, 217T&R, 218-219; **Drucilla Handy Co.:** 100-101; **Nancy Hill Photography:** 105T&C, 114R, 115, 148, 164; **Greg Hursley:** 64-65, 78-79, 80-81, 96-97, 102-103, 180-181, 182, 183R&B, 212, 213, 214, 215, 246, 247T&R, 248, 249; **Jenifer Jordan:** 15T, 68T, 89; **Jerry Jacka:** 6, 7, 10, 11L, 17, 18, 19T, 72-73, 76, 101T, 104, 116, 117B, 119, 120B&C, 124T, 134L, 137L&R, 143, 149L, 161T, 165T&R, 166R, 170B, 173T, 202, 207B, 218; **Jerry Jacka/Arizona State Museum:** 174B; **Jerry Jacka/Colter Bay Indian Arts Museum:** 195B; **Jerry Jacka/Heard Museum:** 36T, 56R, 61T, 67T, 93L, 155R, 162, 166B, 169BR, 170T, 187T; **Kailer-Grant & Associates:** 232-233; **Dick Kaplan/Southwest Sampler:** 49; **Kohler Artist Editions Reveries:** 236; **Jane Lidz:** 109B, 128-129, 196T&L; **Pegg Macy:** 67B; **Herb & Dorothy McLaughlin/Arizona Photographic Associates:** 98T&C, 123, 166L, 187, 221, 254B; **Melabee M. Miller:** 173B, 186, 193; **Terrence Moore:** 7B, 11T, 12L&B, 15L&R, 16R&B, 19, 30, 32T, 35, 48BR, 86T, 92, 93T, 95, 101B, 132, 134R, 160, 161B, 168, 169T, 170-171, 178B, 199L, 204C, 207L, 225TR, TL&BR, 234, 235, 236L, 243L, 244, 244-245; **Stephen S. Myers/International Stock Photography:** 247; **National Upholstering Co.:** 177, 189B, 191T; **The Naturalist:** 189C, 231T; **Mark Nohl/New Mexico Economic & Tourism Department:** 192R; **John Olsen:** 99; **Joanne Pavia:** 86R, 137T; **Gene Peach Photography:** 8B, 9, 51C, 90T, 91, 110T&R, 120T, 127T, 135, 141L, 145B, 146L, 152R; **PhotoEdit:** Leslye Borden: 24T, 133C; Deborah Davis: 36C; Myrleen Ferguson: 107; Tony Freeman: 106TR&B; G.A. Heaviside: 44, 106TL; M. Richards: 174T, Rhoda Sidney: 110L; M. Wallace: 60; Ulrike Welsch: 39L; David Young-Wolff: 165L, 178T; **Bart Prince:** 240, 241; **Tim Street-Porter:** 58-59; **Robert W. Quigley:** 61R, 238-239; **RB Photographic:** 31T, 175, 197; **Reed Bros.:** 32L, 76-77, 188B; **Gail Russell:** 12R; **Santagto:** 63C&B; **Pam Singleton/Image Photography:** 56L, 62, 68B, 82-83, 222, 224, 226L&B, 227, 228-229; **Michael Skott:** 172, 173C, 176-177, 178-179, 183L, 184, 190, 191B, 192L, 198, 200-201; **Beverley Spears:** 195C; **Lawrence J. Speck:** 199R, 225BL; **Thomasville Furniture, Inc.:** 184-185; **David Valenzuela:** 111, 112, 117L, 121, 122-123, 130-131; **Charles L. White:** 75L, 118-119, 125, 138-139, 140, 147, 226R, 230, 252-253; **Mongerson Wunderlich:** 187C, 188T, 189T.

Graphic art courtesy of **Clip Art© 1990 RT Computer Graphics.**

TABLE OF CONTENTS

SOUTHWEST EXPRESSIONS

The dramatic history of the Southwest is transcribed in its rich architectural heritage. Each new wave of settlers, from the first migration of Native Americans to today's influx of Americans from other parts of the country, has left its mark on the architecture of the region. Anasazi cliff palaces built of adobe and stone cling majestically to stupendous caverns. Centuries-old Spanish missions anchor the central business districts of major cities. Ranches dot the wide-open plains, and log houses nestle in mountain nooks among tall pines. A

Florida mansion reinterprets simple adobe forms with rich details obviously influenced by Art Deco. A new home with a breathtaking view of the mountains borrows elements from several Southwest styles, making them seem new again.

The easiest way to understand the Southwest is to think of it as the area of the United States explored and colonized by Spanish adventurers during the sixteenth century. This area extends from Florida to California and from the Rio Grande valley to the mountains of Colorado. When Spanish explorers arrived in North America, they encountered Native Americans who had a highly developed architecture. Although the well-built cities of the Aztecs, Incas, and Pueblos did not prevent the Europeans from conquering them, the Spanish colonists had no choice but to make the pervasive and firmly established native architecture their own. It was simply too appropriate for the region to ignore. The Spanish colonists adopted these building styles to meet their needs

for shelter and security, creating a hybrid architecture that enabled the establishment of missions and presidios (forts) throughout the Southwest.

The powerful and compelling lure of the Southwest began as a Spanish myth of Seven Golden Cities more than 450 years ago and continues to enthrall us. Today the Southwest is the fastest growing region of the United States. Santa Fe style has captured the imagination of people everywhere, and Southwest architecture, furniture, art, clothing, jewelry, and food are now available throughout the country. Even people who have never been in the Southwest are beginning to appreciate the subtle but exciting differences between the regional architectural and life styles of Texas, New Mexico, Arizona, and California.

This book explores the rich diversity of the Southwest, following its main architectural themes as they have developed through the centuries. Along with Spanish colonial and Pueblo influences, Southwest expressions have been shaped by territorial forts, Victorian imports arriving on the transcontinental railroad, the harsh necessities of ranch life, the major themes of modern architecture, and the relaxed, eclectic attitudes of post-modern design.

Spanish Colonial Style

*T*he first Spanish soldiers who explored the Southwest did not find what they were looking for, the fabled Seven Cities of Gold. Rumors of these solid gold cities had begun to circulate among the troops not  long after the conquest of Mexico, but an "eyewitness" report by a slave named Esteban intensified the colonial government's desire to claim the rich booty. Francisco Vásquez de Coronado set out with high hopes, but after traveling as far north as the Rio Grande valley and encountering only poor Pueblo villages, the conquistador returned to Mexico City to report his mission a dismal failure.

It is not the fabled Seven Cities of Gold, but the Montezuma Castle, north of Phoenix, is an American treasure. The five-story pueblo houses seem to grow out of their natural surroundings, a building technique often employed in the Southwest today by contemporary architects.

The Spanish government lost interest in the empire's northern frontier, but the Roman Catholic clergy officials eventually developed a plan to convert the native population to Christianity. In 1598 Juan de Oñate obtained a royal warrant for the province of Nuevo México. With 400 men, women, and children, Oñate ventured north along the Rio Grande to establish the first Spanish colony in the Southwest.

In Nuevo México the colonists found land that resembled parts of their Spanish homeland. The arid terrain supported such hardy vegetation as piñon, juniper, and cedar trees. Water was scarce, but the Europeans copied the Pueblos' careful farming of corn, beans, and squash. The Spanish settlers quickly embraced Pueblo architecture, realizing that dried-clay houses ideally suited the region's broiling summers and bitter winters.

Spanish colonists first built the Mission of San Jerome at Taos Pueblo in 1540, taking their architectural cues from sun-baked clay Pueblo architecture that especially suited the region's climate.

The Santuario Nuestra Senora de Guadalupe was built in Santa Fe shortly after 1795. The pitched-roof church, with three-foot-thick walls recently was given a new skin of hand plastering over adobe stucco. The six-foot-high wall at the entrance of the church gives a good sense of the building's scale.

The Spanish colonists were familiar with adobe. The Moors, who occupied southern Spain for more than 700 years, had introduced this common North African building material to Europe. The Spanish word *adobe* was derived from the Arabic *atob,* which means "sun-dried brick." The Spanish colonists in Nuevo México applied the principles of Renaissance and baroque architecture to adobe, developing the unique architectural style that is best exemplified by the mission churches in the Southwest. The Franciscan friars who oversaw the building of these churches managed to create magnificent structures out of simple materials. They used clever baroque lighting techniques to highlight the missions' altars with shafts of bright daylight and learned to make their structures appear to soar in height by building walls several feet thick. The great weight and lack of compressive strength of adobe prohibit tall structures, but the massive mission churches of New Mexico express an exaggerated verticality because their walls are so thick.

Chile *ristras,* hanging from the roof of the *portal* of the visitors' center at the Tumacacori National Monument, and an old mesquite tree frame the Spanish church, which was completed in 1822. The two-story adobe structure and bell tower, part of the mission founded by Father Kino in 1691, is the site of a colorful fiesta each December.

The sparse interior of the Church of Saint Augustine at Isleta Pueblo, south of Albuquerque, New Mexico, is typical of many mission churches.

The wood-and-tin *reredo* (altar screen) in the Santuario de Chimayo in New Mexico was made by the eighteenth century Mexican master known as Molleno. His nickname, "the chile painter," refers to his affinity for brilliant reds.

A pair of ornamental doors, with carved and painted panels, mark the entrance to the interior of a New Mexican adobe compound.

Pueblos traditionally did not use wooden corbels, but the Spanish colonists relied on wooden architectural elements to support roof beams and evenly distribute the weight of the roof. Metal woodworking tools were unknown to the Pueblos, who used stone axes for chopping and shaping wood. But the crown gave each Franciscan who was sent out to convert Indians ten axes, three adzes, three spades, ten hoes, one medium-sized saw, one chisel, two augers, and one wood plane. He also received a large latch for the church door, two small locks, 12 hinges, and 6,000 nails of various sizes. The friars' tools and hardware quickly transformed traditional Pueblo building techniques, but getting large logs for a church's ceiling beams was always difficult because forests were often as much as ten miles away from the pueblos. The massive logs had to be dragged to the site. Adzes were used to shape the logs into roughly squarish beams that were lifted by ropes on pulleys onto corbels imbedded in the walls.

Often a primitive, rough-hewn double door opens to an interior courtyard landscaped with lush gardens and a beautiful swimming pool. This is the entry to a seventeenth-century home in Santa Fe, one of the city's oldest residences.

Russian artist Nicolai Fechin moved to Taos in 1927. His father was a woodworker, and Fechin was meticulous about the wooden details in the adobe home he built. He blended his own country's style with Spanish colonial motifs. In this small den, Fechin used churches as the models for his highly carved corbels. He worked with the only blacksmith in town to custom design lanterns, fixtures, and hardware.

A graceful spindle bench sits in front of a large arched window in the sunroom of the Taos home designed by Nicolai Fechin in the late 1920s. Behind the twisted wooden columns, which like all the other wood pieces in the house are handcrafted, is a small electric fireplace.

Using basic carpenter's tools, the Spanish colonists and the Pueblo men they had trained as carpenters handcarved door and window frames, doors, *vigas* (roof beams), *zapatas* (corbels), and simple furniture based on medieval and Renaissance forms. Colonial carpenters chipcarved a variety of designs into their woodwork, including rosettes, stars, crosses, animals, and birds. Corbels gave craftsmen an opportunity to show off their considerable skill. This uniquely Spanish architectural detail was strongly influenced by Moorish design. Corbels combine graceful, classical scroll profiles with geometric, stepped, or zigzag cuts. Once the corbel was cut in profile using a saw, the craftsman carved surface designs, notches, lines, or other embellishments. Painting the notches and accents produced elegant results. *Zapatas* are still one of the best-loved features of New Mexico's adobe architecture.

A vintage *trastero* is the unassuming showcase for an *olla* and a *santo* in a Santa Fe adobe abode.

Accommodations for *alfresco* dining long have been integrated into colonial architecture. Here at Alamos, an old silver mining town in Sonora, Mexico, this eighteenth-century sheltered dining room includes a corner fireplace to warm cool evenings.

This Santa Fe entry was crafted in the 1920s by Jose Lopez, one of the most famous New Mexican wood carvers. An angel, birds, trees, and snakes are integrated into the design. Although the Victorian iron chair seems eccentric under the chile *ristras* and against the backdrop of adobe, its curvilinear form and scrollwork seem to echo the forms on the door.

Wooden doors and gates provided wealthy Spanish colonists with greater security and protection against the elements than the Pueblos had enjoyed, but colonists of less wealth continued to use animal hides to cover the entrances to their homes until the early nineteenth century. Colonial doors were fashioned of thick planks, joined by mortises and tenons. Houses built around courtyards during the late eighteenth century usually had a large opening in the exterior wall called a *zaguan.* This opening was secured by a heavy wooden double door called a *portón.* Metal hinges were rare on the frontier, and a *portón* revolved on rounded wooden pegs installed into sockets dug out of the lintel, or cross timber.

Beyond the decorative iron gates is a courtyard at the Heard Museum in Phoenix.

Another colonial architectural invention is the *portal,* which is a porch or covered walkway. The earliest and most celebrated *portal* is the block-long colonnade of the Palace of the Governors in Santa Fe; it was originally built in the early seventeenth century. *Portales* are used as outdoor rooms during the warm months and show great variety and inventiveness. In the most typical design, a series of squared timbers is matched to carved *zapatas* and set in place at regular intervals to support the heavy lintels. The column framework is roofed with small *vigas* and *latillas* (wooden strips or branches) to complete the porch.

The homes built by the colonists in Nuevo México were low and linear, and extended families developed large housing complexes over several generations. Single rooms were added as needed to accommodate a newlywed couple or an aging grandmother. House plans were (and still are) single-file linear, L-shaped, U-shaped, or square with a central patio, or courtyard. Outside walls had few openings, and access into the courtyard was secured by heavy gates.

Tlaquepaque Village in Sedona, Arizona, features *portales* with broad arches, tile roofs, and a fountain in the courtyard. This upscale shopping center also houses restaurants and galleries.

Adobe-brick ranches, like this one in Tucson's desert climate, often are designed around outdoor living. The front of this house is sited to take advantage of a mountain view; the back has French doors that open to a *portal* overlooking the swimming pool.

A *portal,* typical of enclosed walkways that characterize colonial buildings, leads visitors of Phoenix's Heard Museum to a white marble sculpture entitled "Earth Song," by Chiracahua Apache artist Allan Houser. The pottery is Zuni from the turn of the century.

Bancos, or wall benches, fitted with cushions and pillows flank a stepped, elevated fireplace in this adobe home. Lighted *nichos* house artwork, and below the seating are storage bins for logs.

Construction details add beauty to the architecture of Spanish colonial homes, which are spare, utilitarian, and fortified. The inside walls were plastered by hand with colored clays, in cocoa brown, salmon, yellow, or white, often flecked with bits of mica. Finely cut *latillas* made of white aspen or red cedar were laid in a herringbone pattern above the *vigas* to create handsome ceilings. Bell-shaped fireplaces built into the corners of multipurpose living rooms, called the *salas,* reflected a Moorish influence. The Spanish colonists developed the shallow corner fireplaces, which have become an essential architectural element of Southwestern

The *portal* of this home is an inviting spot for *tapas* and margaritas at sunset. The outdoor fireplace adds heat as well as a handsome architectural element. The furnishings are eclectic: wicker seating upholstered in bold stripes, teamed with a contemporary iron-based glass-topped table, on which sit colonial-style brass candlesticks and a woven runner.

One of John Gaw Meem's best-known private homes was completed in 1932. His clients wanted a residence that looked "homemade and informal, not affected or artificial." Meem's design is an unassuming but warm backdrop for the mix of antiques that furnish the room.

architecture. The Pueblos tended fire pits in their houses but did not channel the smoke out of their rooms. Smoke from the fire escaped through an opening in the roof, which also was an entrance to the room. Spanish colonial fireplaces were small earthen hearths. Large *salas* often had two diagonally opposed corner fireplaces. The classic fireplace features an elliptical opening. The firebox itself is shallow, and logs are placed vertically, leaning against each other and the back wall. Some fireplaces are elevated above the floor and united in design with a masonry *banco,* or bench.

Dark-stained wood beams and woodwork contrast with stark white walls to create a strong backdrop for the *sala* in this Paradise Valley, Arizona, home. The fireplace has a striking conical silhouette. The furnishings are a mix of traditional pieces with Southwest art and pottery.

This red Ganado Navajo rug was woven by Sarah Begay.

Weathered wooden gates open to the patio at the Santuario de Chimayo. The church, which was built over a well said to have healing powers, was completed in 1814. In the center of the courtyard is a wagon wheel from an old Mexican pushcart set into an adobe block that also holds a crucifix.

Rebuilding New Mexico

In 1680 the Pueblos of Nuevo México successfully launched an uprising against the Spanish colonists. After driving away their Spanish oppressors, the Pueblos burned and destroyed mission churches, houses, and government buildings. Many Spanish colonists retreated to El Paso; others returned to Mexico. In 1692 Diego de Vargas led a reconquest of the upper Rio Grande.

Many mission churches in New Mexico were beyond repair, but some were rebuilt and have been preserved. Along with more than 100 village and community parishes, the colonial churches and missions of New Mexico form a unique chapter of America's architectural history. The monumental, sculptural simplicity of San Estevan in Acoma Pueblo, the Mission of San Francisco de Asis in Ranchos de Taos, and the Santuario de Chimayo anticipates the aesthetic of stark planar geometry embraced by modern architecture.

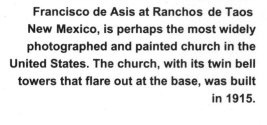

The handsome adobe facade of San Francisco de Asis at Ranchos de Taos New Mexico, is perhaps the most widely photographed and painted church in the United States. The church, with its twin bell towers that flare out at the base, was built in 1915.

The moon rises over the back of the San Francisco de Asis Mission Church. Its stark geometric form embodies an aesthetic embraced by modern architecture.

A side patio of an old adobe home in Phoenix boasts a fountain. Chile *ristras* hang from posts that support the *portal*.

Interior designer Jackie Mallory became smitten with an old adobe home near the Rio Grande in Corrales, New Mexico. The house, which was built in 1920, has two-foot-thick walls and brick floors. Configured like an old hacienda, there are windows on one side that look out to a flagstone courtyard. In her dining room, Mallory teamed a table made from old pine, with ladder-back chairs from Portugal.

The New Mexican colonists perfected a highly successful architectural and ecological response to their adopted homeland. Family compounds, such as the Martinez hacienda built in 1825 in Taos, were self-sufficient and fortified against raids by Apaches and Comanches. Villages were built around contiguous, fortified plazas, along the Rio Grande, Pecos, and Santa Cruz rivers. These towns were centers of trade and culture, but they also offered the best defense against Indian attack.

In 1800 the European population of Santa Fe was close to 4,000 people. Most lived in squat adobe buildings that had been whitewashed. The walls of these houses were about three feet thick. Only the church and the governor's palace had glazed windows. Except around the plaza, the town had a chaotic arrangement of houses and cornfields, with ample space between neighbors to ensure privacy. A poor family's home, called a *jacale,* was only as long as its roof poles that were cut from the small trees that grew near the town. A rich family could hire woodcutters to climb high in the mountains to cut longer poles for their home. In Santa Fe the distinction between rich and poor was obvious, although no one in New Mexico lived as well as colonists in most other parts of the Spanish empire.

The Martinez hacienda in Taos is a restored Spanish colonial fortress with characteristic parapets at the roofline. In the foreground is a large *horno,* or bread-baking oven, introduced to the Pueblos by the Spanish who got it from the Arabs. The oxcart near the entrance is a replica of one used to carry supplies.

The padres' kitchen at San Juan Capistrano Mission shows the melding of Spanish and Pueblo styles that is typical of California missions. The kitchen is in one of the oldest sections of the complex, which dates to about 1786.

The whitewashed walls and packed earth floors of some *jacales* were covered with coarse wool rugs, but beds, tables, and chairs were luxuries that only the rich could afford. People held their plates on their knees when they ate and generally used no tableware other than a spoon. Except that haciendas were also built of adobe, they bore little resemblance to the homes of the poor. Many had ten or more rooms opening onto a central patio. Interior walls were hung with calico, and floors were covered with carpets from Europe. Mattresses were kept rolled against the wall during the day where they served as additional seating, but meals were eaten at the dining table in most haciendas.

While many colonial buildings in remote villages have been lost to weather, depopulation, remodeling, or vandalism, Spanish colonial building principles continue to flourish in New Mexico. The propitious blending of Spanish and Pueblo building techniques has produced a charming and picturesque vernacular architecture, which continues to be reinterpreted in new and exciting ways.

The merging of design styles is evident in this Santa Fe living room, which showcases artist Nicolai Fechin's interpretation of Southwest living. The artist handcarved columns and railings of ponderosa pine; the furniture and doors are clear white sugar pine and poplar. Styles range from rough-hewn *vigas* to a richly ornamental sideboard and column, but the entire house has a Spanish colonial feel.

A cosmopolitan ambience characterizes this Southwest dining room. Large leather-upholstered side chairs have chunky cabriolet legs. They pull up to a table weathered with a milky wash and set with Imari-patterned dinner plates, fine crystal, and formal flatware. The buff-colored walls are defined with a plaster chair rail, painted off-white to match the fireplace. The corners are decorated with iron hardware, which is part of the window treatment.

Arts and Crafts in Colonial Spain

Until the arrival of the Spanish colonists in the Southwest, wooden furniture was unknown. The Pueblos built seating into their kivas, but in their homes they traditionally sat on the floor on piles of boughs and animal skins. The Spanish craftsmen who helped colonize New Mexico and California brought metal woodworking tools with them. In the missions these *carpinteros* taught Native American men to make furniture and wooden architectural embellishments.

The laborious process of building furniture began with felling a tree with an ax or a two-handed bucksaw, or *sierra*. After the branches were removed, the log was brought down from the mountain forest to a mill, where boards were made out of the rough timber. Lumber was planed by hand, and often furniture that was made in the Spanish colonies was somewhat crude, with rough surfaces and massive proportions. Metal fasteners were extremely scarce so most furniture was joined with mortises and tenons. The exposed tenon, coming completely through the mortise, which originally was a structural necessity, has become a signature of Spanish colonial furniture and is often incorporated into reproductions and modern interpretations of the style.

The weaving room at the Martinez hacienda in Taos is dominated by a replica of a Spanish colonial loom. The corner fireplace is the building's only heat source, and the ceiling beams were adzed by hand.

Painted wooden folk art animals by Oaxacan craftsman Manuel Jiminez pop out against a white adobe fireplace, framed with colorful tilework. A large *nicho* was designed as a bookshelf.

Chairs, tables, benches, and chests were the only kinds of furniture produced in the Spanish colonies during the seventeenth century. Chairs and tables were primarily used in churches. Like their Pueblo neighbors, most colonists ate their meals sitting on the floor and holding their bowls in their laps. In some colonial adobes, a bench, or *banco,* was built into the wall, usually near the fireplace. *Bancos* were used for seating and to store the wool sacks and sheepskins on which the colonists slept. *Bancos* have become a familiar feature of Southwest design.

While otherwise devoid of furniture, many colonial homes had a wooden *caja*, or chest, that was used to store clothing and other valuables under lock and key. These simple chests were made of five boards joined at the edges with a hinged top. As the craft of furniture making developed in New Mexico, chests came to be embellished with chipcarved rosettes, crosses, animal motifs, and Moorish designs. During the eighteenth century, more elaborate cupboards were built. *Trasteros* are large upright cabinets, and they usually were richly carved and painted with bright colors.

Square-cut beams bring down the ceiling to give this small alcove a sense of intimacy in the Taos home designed by Nicolai Fechin. The lantern was crafted by a local blacksmith.

Carved redwood, stained a silvery gray, reflects Spanish colonial proportions and styling. These pieces are an elegant addition to the patio of a California adobe, which is paved with terra cotta tiles. The Sonoma lounge chair and ottoman and Carmel picnic bench are from Reed Bros.

Wide Ruins rug by Navajo weaver Bah Yazzie Ashley

A handsome piece of wrought iron, possibly from a gate, found in an antique shop in Santa Fe, displays a collection of riding equipment including spurs, a lariat, and sleigh bells.

Since Spanish colonial culture depended on the horse, it was essential for the colonists to establish blacksmith shops in every village and ranch. Along with supplying tack for *charros* (cowboys) and their horses, smiths made tools, hardware, gates, grillwork, and many kinds of household items. Tinsmiths were responsible for cookware, candelabra, lanterns, and wall sconces. Picture frames made of punched tin became a highly developed art form in New Mexico during the eighteenth century.

Spanish colonial silversmiths taught their trade to Navajos and Pueblos in the Southwest, as their counterparts had taught people in other parts of the empire. Rather than directly imitating Spanish styles of jewelry, these Native American craftsmen developed their own designs that commingle Hispanic filigree with the pattern and imagery seen in Pueblo pottery. Before they were introduced to silver jewelry, the Pueblos made boldly designed jewelry from carved stones and shells, but with the Spanish influence, they developed the stunning worked-silver and turquoise jewelry that continues to be highly valued.

Floral designs have been handtooled on the leather of this padded saddle, which probably was made in Mexico.

This living room at the Inn of the Anasazi is part of a major renovation by the Aspen Group and designers Jim Rimelspach and Susan Seifert of Trisha Wilson & Associates.

Until the arrival of the Spanish colonists, Pueblo weavers had worked with the cotton cultivated in fields near each village. The Spanish colonists introduced sheep into the Southwest, and by the seventeenth century, Pueblo weavers had begun to use wool as well as cotton to make blankets and fabric for clothing. Spanish weavers used large horizontal looms; Native Americans employed simpler upright looms, but there are outstanding similarities in the textiles they produced. The Spanish Rio Grande style of weaving developed alongside Pueblo and Navajo weaving. Until the mid eighteen hundreds, weavers from both cultures used horizontal stripes, but after that many Hispanic blankets have a dominant central medallion or diamond motif. This blanket design was influenced by serapes imported from Saltillo, Mexico, and was eventually adopted by Navajo weavers. Other distinct Hispanic weaving styles developed in the isolated mountain villages of El Valle and Chimayo. El Valle blankets have zigzags or radiant stars, while blankets from Chimayo have stylized thunderbird designs.

Apache baskets

The style that is so characteristic of adobe architecture in the Southwest, the sculpting of *nichos* into walls, is an especially effective device for showing off artwork. Subtle illumination adds to the effect. A pair of tile-decorated *bancos* offer places to sit and enjoy the fire.

Colorful blankets stand out against the clay-colored adobe at Acoma Pueblo.

A pot by Acoma potter Dale Sanchez

Only the front and back walls of the original Mission San Francisco de la Espada in San Antonio, which was rebuilt in 1868, remain. Friars incorporated native Texas limestone into the building, which has a vaulted roof and a tower with three bells. The wooden cross to the side of the door was placed there in 1870, when a prayer for rain was answered.

Texas Missions and Presidios

On the Texas plains, Spanish adventurers encountered a nomadic native population with no permanent architecture. Spanish soldiers, including Cabeza de Vaca and Coronado explored the territory, but colonies were not established in Texas, as they had been in Nuevo México, until after 1684. At that time French colonists under the command of René-Robert Cavelier, Sieur de La Salle, built a fort and colony near Matagorda Bay, 100 miles northeast of Corpus Christi, and the Spanish government became aware of the need to secure its frontier. In 1686 Alonso de León set out from Monterey to find and destroy the French colony. Illness, starvation, and possibly an Indian massacre accomplished the task. When de León found the settlement in April 1689, it was in ruins. There was no actual French presence in Texas, but the fertile plains and seemingly friendly Caddo people encouraged the Spanish government to begin colonizing the area.

This room in the governor's palace has an almost severe look, with its minimal furnishing and wall embellishment.

Spain's first outpost in Texas was established on the Neches River in 1690, but without the threat of French incursion and because of the difficulties of maintaining a garrison in such a remote territory, Spanish soldiers and priests were withdrawn in 1693. For the next 20 years, there was no European presence in the Spanish province. When French soldiers built a fort at Natchitoches in 1714, Spanish authorities responded by building a presidio and mission at San Antonio.

With no native building techniques to imitate and no experienced builders to draft as construction workers, but with a plentiful supply of Texas limestone, the Spanish settlers and friars built mission churches that resembled other Spanish colonial churches. The mission churches of San Antonio, like Mission San Xavier del Bac near Tucson, Arizona, have more in common with the magnificent colonial churches in Mexico than the adobe missions of Nuevo México. Exuberant carved stonework in the heavily ornamented Mexican baroque style adorns these churches. Heavy Texas limestone, sometimes laid in walls up to eight feet thick, makes the missions look like fortresses, which they sometimes became. At San Xavier del Bac, the baroque architectural flourishes hint at Moorish inspirations—a theme that was to be enhanced by architects working in the Spanish colonial style in the twentieth century.

At the back entry to the San Antonio governor's palace is a graceful brick-paved stairway leading to a pantry.

This great room/kitchen is part of a new home in Placitas, New Mexico, designed by Thomas Ashe. There is plenty of counter space, peeled pine beams, carved corbels, *saltillo* tile flooring, and traditional cherry cabinets that have a modern look because the pulls were left off.

40

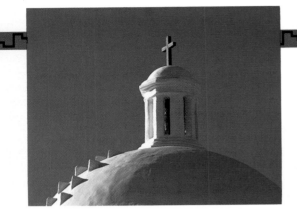

Our Lady of Mount Carmel in Montecito, California, reflects an architectural style developed by missionaries, combining the building patterns of the Pueblo Indians with Spanish colonial design. The plaster walls look like adobe, mimicking the characteristic peachy tan shade.

California Colonial

Spanish colonists did not begin to settle California until after 1769, when Don Gaspar de Portola and Padre Junépero Serra established a mission in San Diego. The Spanish government's jealous rivalry with the French in Florida, Texas, and along the Mississippi had consumed many resources of the waning empire, but once the colonization of California began, it moved quickly. By 1823 there were 21 missions, and about 3,000 Europeans were living in California. Presidios had been built at San Diego, Santa Barbara, Monterey, and San Francisco.

When Spanish colonists first arrived in California, they found a large population of Native Americans, which was soon decimated by epidemics of smallpox and influenza. Intent on converting the maximum number of people to Christianity, the friars enforced the settlement of Native Americans in or immediately around their missions. This large and essentially captive labor force allowed the missions to develop into huge industrial complexes. Missions boasted gardens, grain fields, great herds of livestock, weaving rooms, vineyards, tanneries, blacksmith shops, and warehouses.

The mission at Santa Barbara, California, is an elegant interpretation of colonial style. The facade, based on the work of M. Vieruvius Polion, a Roman architect, follows a pedimented Greek temple form with Ionic columns. At the corners of the triangular pediment, which is delineated with dentil work, are statues representing Faith, Hope, and Charity. Inside the triangle is a statue of St. Barbara.

San Xavier del Bac is called the White Dove of the Desert. The architecture, an arresting combination of Moorish, Byzantine, and Mexican-baroque styles, is the finest example of Spanish-mission architecture in the Southwest. The main entrance is embellished with highly ornamental carvings that have been further enriched with polychrome painting.

43

San Juan Battista

The Franciscans developed an extremely successful plan for establishing a mission. With a small amount of up-front money, a missionary could purchase bells, vestments, seeds, and tools. Other missions contributed what they could, with grants of breeding stock, plant cuttings, and food. After building a crude chapel and a house of logs and brush, the friar began to proselytize the local Chuciscan people. Gifts of glass beads, blankets, and food helped him get his message across. Once a person agreed to become Christian, he or she was not allowed to leave the mission without permission. Spanish soldiers enforced this edict. The new converts were put to work in the fields; as their number grew, they were required to build permanent buildings and were eventually taught the trades necessary to maintain a semblance of European life.

The white adobe mission at San Luis del Ray in Oceanside, California, reflects the marriage of Spanish, Moorish, and Pueblo architecture. Completed in 1850, most of it was restored in 1893. The skull and cross set into the niche of the cemetery gate was added in the 1950s, when the location was used for Zorro movies.

All 21 missions in California followed the same architectural plan, but many of the exteriors are distinguished from one another by certain details, such as the balcony and the blue domed tower here at the Tarzana mission.

The central patio, which anchored most California missions, is a feature borrowed from Moorish architecture. This is the center quadrangle of San Juan Capistrano, renowned for the legend of the swallows, which are said to have returned to the site annually on Saint Joseph's Day.

The friars built their missions around a central patio, copying a primary design feature of Moorish buildings in southern Spain. The extended eaves of the buildings created a covered arcade around the patio. These arcades are often supported by rounded arches, which are typical of Roman architecture in Spain and other parts of the ancient Roman Empire. The thick adobe walls are similar to those built by Pueblos in New Mexico. Heavy red tile roofs, with Mediterranean origins, complete the architecture of the California missions.

Because of their late construction, their vast size, and the rapid settlement of the region after the Gold Rush of 1849, the Spanish missions of California have been preserved, becoming prized landmarks. The fundamental characteristics of California mission architecture, including arcades surrounding patios or gardens, clay-tiled roofs, white stucco walls, and terraced bell towers with domes, have become part of the California architectural vocabulary.

The old Serra Chapel at San Juan Capistrano, built in 1777, is the only structure to have withstood the 1812 earthquake. Its mission architecture became the fashionable vernacular for Southwest buildings. The bell wall was erected after the earthquake. It holds the damaged bells that were dug out of the rubble.

Bougainvillea frame the rounded arches that make up one of the *portales* of San Juan Capistrano. The arches recall Roman architecture in Spain. The colonnade is one of six covered walkways in the complex.

47

Beyond a Spanish colonial gate at El Pueblo, a shopping center in Scottsdale, is a courtyard with a historically correct gazebo.

A New California Style

Around the turn of the twentieth century, the push for statehood in Arizona and New Mexico was causing many citizens of these territories to attempt to cover up their unique history. Many New Mexicans embellished their adobe homes with wallpaper and ornate woodwork, attempting to become more "American" by adopting East Coast design styles. At the same time Pueblo and Spanish colonial influences were disappearing from the Southwest, California designers were beginning to find inspiration in the Spanish missions. A transplanted Yankee, Charles Lummis, became the most vocal advocate for a unique Californian style.

Lummis graduated from Harvard in 1881, but he found that direct experiences of nature and human culture were his best teachers. In 1884 Lummis walked from Cincinnati to Los Angeles, sending off stories to newspaper editors along the way. His travels and adventures in New Mexico among the Pueblos and Hispanic *penitentes* changed his life and provided Lummis with material for his book *The Land of Poco Tiempo.* The book, which was illustrated with drawings, photographs, and engravings, achieved nationwide popularity. Many people got their first introduction to the then largely unknown Southwest by reading Lummis's personal adventures.

Draperies frame an unusual towering bay window in an adobe home. The formality of the window treatment contrasts with the rustic personality of the heavy-beamed ceiling. Furnishings are transitional, neutral pieces. The patterned chairs seem to echo the design from a Navajo rug that hangs on the wall. A collection of pots is displayed throughout the room.

Hopi polychrome ancestral pot

This San Antonio home was inspired by the homeowner's world travels. Chris Carson and Caroline Peterson of the architectural firm Ford, Powell and Carson built the stucco home with native materials in a style that is Roman, Spanish, and New Mexican.

The southern end of the Serra Chapel, the oldest building in continuous use in California, adjoins the bell wall. Padre Junepero Serra said mass here.

Castaneda Hotel, Las Vegas, New Mexico

By 1885 Lummis had become a writer for the *Los Angeles Times.* He used this forum to argue for a unique California culture. The California missions, Lummis wrote, "are worth more than money. They are a greater asset to Southern California than our oil, our oranges, or even our climate."

During the 1890s the mission style began to dominate new construction in California. Executives of the Santa Fe Railroad chose the mission style for the company's depots, and hotelier Fred Harvey built lavish mission hotels to complement the stations. By 1898 the mission-style Castaneda Hotel had been built in Las Vegas, New Mexico, and the even grander Alvarado Hotel in Albuquerque was begun in 1901.

Railroad depot, Santa Fe, New Mexico

Mission Style

The Craftsman, a monthly magazine published by cabinetmaker Gustav Stickley from 1901 to 1916, encouraged straightforward and honest design. Craftsman houses were planned and built to be durable as well as harmonious with their natural settings. Some homes pictured in the magazine were derived from the California mission style, but many were examples of other regional styles of architecture. A mission home pictured in the January 1904 issue of the magazine had thick cement walls, which were left rough and colored in creamy tones, and a low-pitched roof with strong projection, covered with unglazed red Spanish tile. Simplicity of building materials, the use of construction features as the only decoration, and the choice of colors harmonious with the house and its surroundings are the primary features of Craftsman homes of every style. These qualities are particularly effective in mission designs.

Railroad depot, Kingman, Arizona

El Alisal, the home of Charles Lummis, was built between 1897 and 1920. Its structure combines field stone, granite, and timber, some of which came from California missions.

Craftsman furniture, which is now also called mission furniture (although Stickley personally hated the term), was simply made of solid oak in handsome proportions and appropriately accented by leather, wrought metals, or beveled glass panes. Stickley intended to make furniture that "substitutes the luxury of taste for the luxury of costliness." He also published hundreds of plans so that home craftsmen could make their own furniture in his simple, straightforward style. The mass and line of Craftsman furniture is ideally suited to Spanish colonial revival interiors. Although original Stickley pieces have become collectible and expensive, L. & J.G. Stickley is back in business reissuing old designs, and many other companies have begun producing reproductions and reinterpretations of mission furniture and accessories.

Built-in cabinets show the same attention to detail as the other millwork in the Lummis house. Carving on the upper cabinet doors was achieved with a special chisel that Lummis himself fashioned. Along with the rich abundance of millwork, details in stucco, such as the small *nichos,* also were integrated into the design.

Handcrafted window made of redwood, pine, poplar, and maple

The warmth of handcrafted wood abounds throughout the Lummis home. Furnishings are simple and honestly crafted, reflecting Lummis's belief that a man's home should be part of himself. "It should be enduring and fit to endure; life and death will hallow it; it will mellow with the generations—if it outlives them. It should be good architecture, honest construction, comfortable." The ironwork, locks, hinges, and keys came from the collection of artifacts Lummis gathered during travels to Peru and across North America.

This home in Encanto Palmcroft, a historic district of Phoenix, shows Spanish colonial influence with its red tile roof, balcony, and spindle columns.

Spanish Eclecticism

Before California was engulfed by the Spanish colonial revival, architects began to explore the possibilities offered by modern architecture. Irving Gill built streamlined houses and public buildings in Los Angeles and San Diego. Gill simplified California mission style to its most essential forms: clean arcades and pure white walls. In Pasadena Charles Sumner Greene and his brother Henry Mather Greene championed the Arts and Crafts movement and produced remarkable houses and furniture. Greene and Greene blended their mastery of California redwood and intricate Japanese joinery to produce fully design-integrated houses of unique style. Greene and Greene furniture pieces are among the most treasured classics of twentieth-century American furniture design and are appropriate accents in most Southwest interiors.

By 1920 the popularity of the mission style was waning, but architects in California and Florida continued to use and redefine elements of Spanish colonial architecture. The 1915 Panama-Pacific Exposition in San Diego marks the beginning

The Meadows Hotel in Las Vegas, New Mexico, epitomized the flourishes of Spanish design that characterize mission style. Polychrome decorations and bands define the arches and windows, and the tower is especially rich in decoration.

A San Francisco stucco expresses many of the architectural features resulting from cultural crossbreeding, joining a Spanish colonial balcony and spindles, Moorish windows, and a gabled roof of Spanish tile.

The plaster frieze set into the wall of this home in Placitas, New Mexico, suggests a distinct Moorish influence. Not all the embellishments added by designer Thomas Ashe are purely decorative. Just below the *vigas* is a special beam inserted to support the roof during an earthquake.

Since ceilings are low and rooms are small in this old adobe home in Scottsdale, designer Nancy Kitchell maintained a visual levity by painting the walls white, bleaching out the ceiling beams, and upholstering a sofa and wing chairs in a textured white cotton damask.

Interior designer Linda Robinson added color to update this home, designed by architect Josias Joesler in the early 1950s.

of this design trend. Architect Bertram Goodhue designed the exposition's main building in an eclectic evocation of Spanish architecture. The Spanish colonial revival style enjoyed widespread popularity in some of the Southwest's most fashionable communities. Clay-tiled roofs and arcades, and white stucco facades dot the hillsides of Hollywood, Beverly Hills, Bel Air, Santa Monica, and Malibu. The rise of movie stars to fame and fortune in the 1920s was a boon to Spanish colonial architecture in California. So many stars celebrated their new prosperity with lavish Spanish colonial mansions that the style became synonymous with glamour. Many of these grand mansions, as well as thousands of smaller homes, commercial buildings, hotels, and even gas stations, remain from this period.

Entire communities, most notably Santa Barbara, have adopted the Spanish style of the 1920s as their trademark. This interpretation of the Spanish colonial style is eclectic and picturesque. It shares more elements with the Queen Anne style in its complex asymmetry and roof shapes than it shares with the simple adobes of the colonial period. The elaborate baroque details that are found on some colonial church facades, especially in Mexico, have been adapted for door surrounds; wrought iron and richly carved wooden details embellish many surfaces.

Special Touches

The dining room of this Santa Fe home was created by Los Angeles designer Hutton Wilkinson. To recreate the feel of authentic adobe, he added saffron pigment to the wet plaster before it was applied to the walls. The hand-trowled plaster dried unevenly, creating the charming mottled coloring. The distinctive chandelier and matching wall sconces are bronze with dangling Venetian-glass baubles; they came from Lucian's Antiques in Carmel, California. Glazed ceramic pots from Morocco stand guard on either side of a traditional corner fireplace with a raised hearth.

The long refectory table is French provincial, and the Queen Anne chairs, which have been elegantly upholstered in red suede, are a charming foil to the massive table. The sunny fabric of the curtains, which is also French, helps to enhance the room's unexpected lightness, as do the stripped and bleached pine-log *vigas.*

A simple doorway acquires special charm when it is accented with a shapely terra-cotta vase and tin-framed *retablo.* Other folk-art treasures and favorite collectibles, mostly from Mexico, line bright yellow shelves, creating the kind of Southwest pastiche that can bring *salsa* style to any home.

Spanish Colonial Architecture Today

Even after its heyday in the years between the world wars, the Spanish colonial revival style never lost favor with Southwestern builders. The style successfully competed for clients with modernism and other revival styles. With the rise of postmodern architecture in the 1980s, the Spanish colonial design vocabulary took on new vigor, especially in California's coastal cities. Today many of California's leading architects are reinventing the centuries-old Spanish style.

The style's basic building blocks have remained constant—stucco walls, Mexican tile pavers, California clay roof tiles, and handsome interior ceiling beams. The familiar wall colors, including white, Naples yellow, ocher, and sand, continue to be used. Coral and pink exterior stucco are now the preferred hues, while white was popular in the 1920s.

The architectural styling of this house—adobe construction with a pitched tile roof, second-story balcony, and Spanish detailing, such as the tile framing the paneled door, is typical of the hybrid known as Monterey style.

This curved terrace, in a home in Castle Pine, Colorado, designed by Ford, Powell and Carson, extends from a large living room that partially faces into a valley and steps down to a garden below.

Architect Rob Wellington Quigley designed this San Diego residence in the Spanish colonial style, with a courtyard orientation, columned loggia, California clay roof, and arches. The building has a striking contemporary attitude as well, which accounts for some of the choices of materials, such as pipe railings instead of wrought iron. The homeowners wanted the feeling of a Moorish compound, and the architecture suggests a clean interpretation, with its straight-lined gate to the central courtyard, which frames a pair of columns sheathed in copper.

In this Scottsdale, Arizona, guest house, architect Adolf deRoy Mark designed a storage banquette that reflects the stylized Southwest forms used throughout the home. The cabinet is rough-sawn wood, stained blue and finished with simple hardware. The piece houses a sink with a tiled backsplash, a television, and drawers for clothing. On the other side of the pedimented temple is the bathroom.

Today's designs for Spanish colonial homes have radically different floor plans and elevations than earlier designs. Architects continue to use such major design elements as rounded and square towers, exaggerated baroque windows, courtyards, fountains, and fancy entrance gates, but they are now assembled dramatically along diagonal axes rather than simple, traditional horizontals and verticals. A new California Spanish house may cling to a hillside overlooking the Pacific or provide an expansive architectural bridge across a canyon.

Talented designers have recaptured the glory of the great ranches of early California in new colonial haciendas. Zigzag terraces and stairways provide a fascinating relationship between the house and its site, in the spirit of colonial patios and courtyards. Elegant arcades are flattened, bisected, rotated, abstracted, and joined to walls in unusual angles. Subtle, sophisticated, and often daring window compositions punctuate walls in unpredictable ways. California's postmodern Spanish style promises to become a major design statement.

A traditional beehive fireplace interpreted differently by architect Wayne Lloyd

Although it is just a few years old, this home outside Phoenix inherits many elements from Spanish-colonial architecture. The house is situated around a courtyard, with its *portal* wrapping around the swimming pool. A bubbling fountain and waterfall are some of the features that landscape designer Ron Ackerlund built into the garden, in which he used indigenous plants such as Palo Verde trees.

In the foyer to a Santa Fe adobe condominium, architect Wayne Lloyd cut into the *viga* ceiling to open the house to the sky.

Texas Hacienda

On a large working ranch of several thousand acres, 30 miles from the Rio Grande in south Texas, architect David Lake of Lake/Flato incorporated a pair of stucco buildings from the 1970s into a complex that recalls a Spanish hacienda. The original main house and guest quarters were gutted, and a master bedroom, game room, and guest extension were added. Many of the architectural references are very specific: The homeowner was fond of the nineteenth-century brick buildings in two nearby towns, Roma and Rio Grande City, and many of the features of particular buildings were integrated into those of the compound.

The compound is a series of independent buildings, each with its own character, details, and colors. "It was like designing a small town," says Lake. One huge grassy courtyard with covered porches is the central link. Walls were built with irregular Mexican brick. The pedimented building is the master bedroom suite. Louvre doors lead to the courtyard.

A breezeway connects the guest wing to the master suite. On this side of the house, there is a distant view of the pasture. The guest tower is a simple rectangle, detailed with recessed squares. The design was inspired by a particular building in Roma.

Territorial Style

*T*he nineteenth century brought dramatic changes to the Southwest; it was a time of conflict, expansion, and discovery. New Mexico broke free of Spanish dominance, Santa Fe became what it still is—a romantic trad-  ing post in the high desert, and California and Texas were quickly settled by Yankees and became states in the Union. Covered wagons from the East began regularly to cross the plains, and the American army soon followed to protect traders and settlers from Indian raids. Railroads were built across the Southwest and with them came new cities and towns, built of clapboard and brick.

Bougainvillea frames the entrance to this Palm Springs ranch, which was built in 1926. Decorative wrought-iron security bars are attached to simple window frames, the upper portions applied like lintels. The vintage wagon wheel was left behind by a former owner.

A Year of Destiny

In August 1821 Juan O'Donoju, the commanding Spanish general, signed the Treaty of Cordoba, officially ending Spanish rule over New Spain. The treaty created the short-lived, independent Mexican Empire; this government was replaced within three years by the Mexican Republic made up of 19 states and four territories, which included Nuevo México, Alta California, and Texas.

The year 1821 also saw the first arrival of traders from Missouri in Santa Fe. William Becknell had set out from Independence to trade with the Comanches, but he changed his plans and arrived in Santa Fe with a small supply of cloth and metal tools. After realizing an extraordinary profit on the goods he sold, Becknell established a trade route from Missouri to New Mexico, which became known as the Santa Fe Trail.

French doors were added to the skinny dining room in this 60-year-old adobe home in Palm Springs. The cement slab floor was painted white and the walls whitewashed to enhance the space. The furnishings are an explosion of color and whimsy that often signal Southwest style: iron chairs upholstered in patterned Guatemalan fabric, an iron table with an etched-glass top, a cedar-twig screen painted by the homeowner, and a pair of totem poles by Santa Fe artist Dick Jemison. Homeowner Arthur Coleman made the moon-shaped metal lamp and the life-size photographic cutout of a cowboy.

From his second floor apartment in Phoenix, designer Craig Pearson enjoys great views. "It's like living in a tree house," he says. But with only 600 square feet, Pearson had to maximize the space. He combined patterns connected by their earthy hues. To frame the big windows, Pearson hung fabric from leather straps on old railroad spikes.

During 1821 Moses Austin and his son Stephen got permission from the new government in Mexico to establish a colony in Texas on the banks of the Brazos River. By 1830, when Antonio López de Santa Anna, the president of Mexico, closed the border to further Yankee immigration, 30,000 United States immigrants were living in Texas.

During the early 1820s, regular trade between California and the East Coast began. *Vaqueros* (cowboys) developed a successful trading partnership with Boston merchants. The "Bostons" bought hides from California ranches, shipped them around Cape Horn, and then sold them to boot and shoe factories in New England. The going rate was one dollar per hide. Trade in hides soon led to trade in many other goods, and even before the Gold Rush, California was importing many things from the United States.

The only change made in the living room of this Palm Springs adobe was the sandblasting of the beamed ceiling, which had been stained dark. Designer Carla Kalwaitis mixed an old sofa, which was refinished and upholstered in Brindle cowhide (a skin with spots), with vintage pieces; a horn chair; and contemporary artwork. The rug is crafted from leather strips. The rustic pine cubbyholes flanking the fireplace are used for storage and to house a television.

Lonely Dell Ranch at Lee's Ferry, Arizona

Texas: An American Outpost

In Texas, which remained a Mexican territory until 1836, the rapid influx of new settlers never allowed a true marriage of Anglo and indigenous architecture. Moses Austin's new village on the Brazos (now called Austin) boasted sturdy log cabins from its beginnings. By 1845 when Texas became part of the United States, many wooden frame buildings graced the hillsides of the new Texas capital.

Log cabins and frame structures were built in most parts of territorial Texas, except in San Antonio and the lower Rio Grande valley, where architecture remained much the same as it had been during the Spanish colonial era. In that area prominent landowners lived in spacious stone houses with flat roofs; *rancheros* lived in modest adobe houses; and laborers lived in *jacales*, which are houses made of mud, branches, and thatched roofs.

After the Civil War, San Antonio still looked like a Mexican town, in spite of its cosmopolitan population of 12,000 French, German, American, and Mexican residents. German immigrants in particular brought touches of their homeland to Texas. In 1857 an observer described a cottage in New Braunfels as a "long room . . . the walls pink, with stenciled panels, and scroll ornaments in crimson, and neatly framed . . . lithographic prints hanging on all sides."

The living room of this classic whitewashed adobe in Phoenix features *saltillo* tiles, arched doorways, and a stepped partial room divider. The furnishings are a mix of transitional and traditional. Such juxtapositions of architecture and design elements as the fine porcelain piece displayed in the *nicho* are uniquely Southwest.

The upstairs parlor at the Cooper-Molera house in Monterey reflects a mix of furnishings. The table in the foreground is an early motion picture device; its circular top spins like a lazy Susan.

California Adobes

The Spanish colonists and friars who built the California missions introduced adobe architecture to the region. Early California seaports and ranches mimicked the style of the missions. These California adobes built before 1820 resembled buildings in New Mexico, following a linear floor plan, with massive walls, an attached wooden *portal,* or porch, a flat roof, and simple door and window openings. The walls usually were whitewashed, but sometimes exposed adobe walls were decorated by pressing small colored stones or seashells into wet bricks or mortar in decorative patterns.

Monterey and Santa Barbara boast many fine examples of a charming blend of Spanish colonial and New England architecture that relates to the hybrid territorial architecture of New Mexico. In stark contrast to booming San Francisco, an 1853 lithograph of Los Angeles shows a quiet plaza surrounded by adobe houses of one and two stories, many with flat roofs and *portales.*

As early as 1800, California builders had begun making clay roof tiles. These tiles were 16 inches across and molded around wooden forms into uniform curved shapes that fit together to make a weather-resistant roof. Clay-tiled roofs were a distinguishing characteristic of both California territorial and Spanish colonial architecture. A fundamental difference between New Mexico and California territorial architecture was the roof structure. Buildings in New Mexico retained the flat, mud-packed roofs of Pueblo construction

Casa Soberanes in Monterey dates to about 1845, when it was built by a half brother of Governor Juan Estrada, whose family lived there from 1860 to 1922. The mullion windows give a territorial flavor to this California adobe.

Like many of its contemporaries built in the late 1820s, the Cooper-Molera house in Monterey combines traditional adobe architecture with Yankee notions about furnishing interiors. This home was restored to reflect its appearance in 1845.

until the introduction of corrugated tin roofs in the 1860s, while the Californios built simple gable, shed, or hip roofs to support curved clay roof tiles.

After the port of Monterey was opened to foreign trade in 1822, Yankee merchants and craftsmen began arriving in California. They quickly influenced adobe construction. Instead of the traditional linear plan, the Americans built their houses two rooms deep and sometimes two stories high. A central interior staircase gave access to the upper floor. On top of their squarish houses, the new arrivals built hipped roofs, often crowned with wooden shingles. The attractive addition of graceful two-story wooden verandas or cantilevered balconies created a private outdoor sitting area, with access from the second story. Carpenters delighted in embellishing these porches. Styles ranged from simple rough-cut posts to classical chamfered columns and fancy Victorian millwork. Elaborate corbels, like those found in New Mexico, were rare in California, where carpenters concentrated on decorating the verandas of the haciendas they built.

The patio of the Heard Museum in Phoenix

San Antonio Ranch Style

A *portal* protects a home from the heat and creates a wonderful place from which to view the garden. In Texas the western sun is unforgiving, so this San Antonio ranch, designed by architect John Grayble, features a series of wraparound verandas that capture the prevailing breezes. The home, which was built of limestone and rough-hewn timber, is a series of inter-locking structures.

The veranda on the west facade announces the kitchen and breakfast wing. The columns are 12 inches square; the depth of the porch is ten feet, almost room-size.

The homeowner is fond of antiques, and one of her requisites for designing the kitchen was to incorporate an old oak haberdashery storage unit into the plan. The generously apportioned kitchen is anchored by a center island, which has a pullout marble insert and sink, and an overhead rack for pots and pans. The commercial range was actu-ally built into a fireplace, so that all the hot air from cooking goes up the chim-ney. The tile that surrounds the oven and decorates the backsplash and countertops is from Portugal. The cap on the cabinets provides a ledge for displaying plates and baskets.

A Garden Escape

Enormous boulders were imported courtesy of the Texas highway department, which was building new roads on the outskirts of town. They were integrated into the landscaping and stacked using a German smear technique. Warm tones of cement were blended with the color of the stone. As the architect puts it, "You don't get a peanut brittle look." The effect is an organic composition and the appearance that the stone walls sprung from the ground. A hot tub, with direct access from the master bedroom, sits at the top of the steps. The roofing on the house is seamed metal, a material introduced to the Southwest by American soldiers.

In the Southwest the back of a home is often more open and inviting than the front. Oriented toward a landscaped garden and pool, the back of this Texas house has sheltering verandas that naturally cool the interior.

California Territorials

As soon as American traders began arriving in California and New Mexico, they influenced the traditional functions of rooms. The multipurpose rooms of the colonial period gave way to rooms with specialized uses, such as parlors, dining rooms, and bedrooms, and in some lavish homes, music rooms and libraries. Territorial houses in California also extended their living spaces into the outdoors to take advantage of the pleasant climate and beautiful vegetation. Courtyards, patios, and formal gardens were included in the plans of most mid-nineteenth-century haciendas.

Many of the first Americans in California were New England traders, and their taste in interior furnishings transformed the sparse interiors of the Spanish colonial period. Wallpaper was introduced into Monterey in the 1830s, and soon prosperous merchants were importing the currently popular styles of East Coast wall coverings. Unlike New Mexicans, who could import only a limited amount of American furniture overland on the Santa Fe Trail, Californians shipped impressive quantities of home furnishings on the high seas. Pianos, sideboards, secretaries, poster beds, and great dining tables graced homes in the bustling port of Monterey.

Pacific House in Monterey was built by Thomas Larkin in 1847 for use by the army.

The owners of this Southwest stucco home in Scottsdale, Arizona, live in New Jersey. When they furnished their desert digs, they told designer Paula Berg that they wanted the house to reflect the relaxed lifestyle they enjoy in Arizona. Berg responded with an eclectic mix of furnishings in a blending of styles that is both casual and dressy. The dining room's iron fixture was made by Bruce Eicher.

New Mexico Territorial Style

Between 1820 and 1860, Yankee traders and the U.S. Army had an enormous impact on architectural styles in the Southwest, producing a hybrid fashion, now known as territorial style. By 1850 Texas (1845) and California (1850) had joined the Union, but the territorial period of New Mexico's history had just begun. In 1847, after troops under the command of General Zachary Taylor and General Winfield Scott drove Mexican forces out of California and the Southwest and captured Mexico City, the Mexican government ceded all its land north of the Rio Grande to the United States. New Mexico now became a United States territory and trade along the Santa Fe Trail expanded rapidly, despite threats of attack from Comanches, Kiowas, and Apaches. In 1852 the Army built Fort Union in northeast New Mexico, near the junction of the Mountain and Cimarron branches of the Santa Fe Trail. The garrison at the fort safeguarded the trail's commerce, and Fort Union became the supply center for the entire network of forts in the Southwest.

The territorial style brings together Greek revival elements blended with adobe construction at Ft. Union in northeast New Mexico. The squat mud-brick structures had pedimented wooden windows and casings with double-hung sashes.

Designer Carla Kalwaitis played up contrasts in textures with white eyelet and Battenberg lace bed linens, juxtaposed with textural brick adobe, rustic pine built-ins, twig furniture, and a traditional corner fireplace. The cow skull over the fireplace is bronze plated.

Beneath the *vigas* in this territorial adobe in La Mesilla, New Mexico, is an eighteenth-century Virginia rope bed, graced with a quilt made by the homeowner's mother in 1939. The fan-shaped window has a deep recess, which allows a window seat. The recessed area on the bed wall displays a collection of *santos*.

East of the Mississippi River, the peace and prosperity of the new nation helped to make Greek revival architecture and design popular. Starting in the early 1800s, the formal elegance of Greek motifs was favored for public buildings, especially courthouses and city halls, and the grand homes of Southern plantation owners. When Fort Union was expanded in 1862, Greek revival architectural details and house plans were adapted to adobe construction. This hybrid style became known as New Mexico territorial.

Army carpenters and masons invented and crafted details never before seen in the Southwest. Instead of hand-hewn *portal* supports, territorial porch columns were squared off, then chamfered at the corners. Applied trim moldings formed simple capitals and bases. Instead of rough window and door openings, Fort Union boasted precisely framed windows and doors with elongated proportions. Double-hung sash

Simplicity is perhaps the most compelling feature of this dining room, which is part of a guest house in Santa Fe that dates to the late 1700s. The furnishings show the mix of styles that became part of Southwest culture with Yankee influence. The library table is English and the chairs are from Seret & Sons, a local furnishings dealer. The only pattern in the room comes from an antique Oriental rug.

Chile *ristras* hang from the eaves of the roof of Rancho de Chimayo. The trio of pedimented, double-hung windows and the gabled roof show the evolution of architectural style.

windows and elegant panelled doors surrounded by sidelights, as well as transom windows flooded rooms at the fort with bright sunlight. Pedimented lintels, crowning the tops of window and door frames, added a hint of Greek temple ornamentation, and have become a trademark of the territorial style. Unlike earlier buildings, territorial adobes rested on a solid foundation of brick or stone masonry, and the tops of the buildings featured brick coping, as a simplified evocation of a classical entablature.

The Spanish colonial preference for linear house plans was modified by territorial builders into a symmetrical plan of two rooms on either side of a central hallway. One front room served as a parlor, the other as a master bedroom. A children's bedroom and a kitchen-dining room took up the back of the house. The large central hallways, which could be 14 feet wide, were used for dances and parties.

The army introduced many new building materials into the Southwest. Hard-fire bricks and lime for mortar and plaster gave territorial adobes a sharper profile. Sheets of tin and zinc covered soggy earthen roofs. Gleaming white paint on porches, doors, and windows, accented by forest green window shutters, enhanced the classical illusion of the somewhat squat buildings.

The window boxes on this house on Canyon Road in Santa Fe have been planted with petunias and geraniums, which dress up the territorial window. The white frame complements both the adobe and the flowers.

A massive stone fireplace adds coziness to this Palm Springs adobe. The furnishings are eclectic: a willow bench, a Ralph Lauren rattan sofa, an unusual white-ground Indian blanket, a stone table with a metal base, and a wrought-iron fixture that was original to the house. The pedimented lintels above the window and door frames are hallmarks of territorial style.

Wisps of salmon hollyhocks soften the adobe building that houses Nedra Matteucci Fine Arts on Canyon Road in Santa Fe. The territorial window, with its simple pedimented crown, has been painted an electric cobalt blue.

New Mexican Classics: The Great Haciendas

Between 1850 and 1880, many enterprising entrepreneurs and ranchers made large fortunes on the New Mexican frontier. These men were Santa Fe Trail traders, sheep and cattle ranchers, land barons, and suppliers of the military. Jose Albino Baca, Charles Ilfeld, Willie Spiegelberg, Lucien B. Maxwell, Christopher "Kit" Carson, Samuel Watrous, and the Romero Brothers of Las Vegas prospered during this period before the coming of the transcontinental railroad, which was soon to dominate New Mexico commercially. These men and their families left behind an architectural legacy of great haciendas in which wealth, style, and ambition combined to create a unique grandeur.

The Greek revival styling at Fort Union was adapted for haciendas. The most telling feature of territorial style was the pedimented lintel, a triangular piece of wooden trim used to crown doorways and windows, simplistically evocative of the

An adobe on San Francisco Street in Santa Fe is painted ocher, one of the earth tones that is acceptable in the historic area.

The courtyard at the Hyatt Gallery on Upper Canyon Road in Santa Fe has an iron gate, arched entries, a fountain, and decorative Mexican tile, suggesting that the exterior architecture and grounds were given as much consideration as the interior.

classical pediment of Greek architecture. The amount of carved molding applied to a lintel implied the wealth and status of its owner. In most houses the elaborately carved corbels of the colonial period were now abandoned in favor of simple molded trim on capitals and bases. White paint applied to columns and window frames created a crisp, formal harmony.

The great territorial mansions built after 1850 featured a dramatic extension of rooms upward to two stories of adobe. The Baca mansion in Las Vegas (1855) even had a third, attic story. A hacienda's front facade might have boasted a double *portal* of symmetrically placed posts, and the house was usually capped by a simple wooden or terneplate-sheathed gable roof. The overall effect was an elegant, classically ordered block not unlike an antebellum plantation house in the South.

One territorial adaptation of adobe interiors was the addition of an Anglo-style mantel to an adobe fireplace. This mantel in a Santa Fe adobe is an antique, carved from a single piece of hand-pegged pine.

The focal point of this room is a modern variation of a shepherd's fireplace, which dates to the latter part of the nineteenth century. The adobe fireplace features a deck as part of its construction, once used for sleeping to take advantage of the heat created beneath. The wooden legs and framework also are typical, although this fireplace has a distinctive primitive design. The furnishings are contemporary, anchored by a glass-topped table. The *vigas* are embellished with hand-painted ribbons.

The kitchen of Kit Carson's house in Taos, which was built in 1825, is typical of the times. Bowls and clay pots sit on a pair of pine shelves. Below the shelves is a strip fitted with dowels that is handy for hanging aprons. There are plenty of places to hang corn or herbs for drying. A copper oil lamp, suspended above the pine table, belonged to the Carson family.

On Canyon Road in Santa Fe, where many art galleries are located, some woodwork is fancifully painted. This territorial door is embellished with colorful zigzags, the kind that you might find on a Navajo rug.

Other haciendas were built by men who supplied cattle and grain to the Army. Samuel Watrous began trading near Fort Union in 1849. His house was strategically located at La Junta, the junction of the Mountain and Cimarron branches of the Santa Fe Trail. Over time his house grew to 26 rooms, surrounding a courtyard. Since the Watrous house was the first hacienda that wagon trains encountered after crossing hundreds of miles of buffalo grass, it must have been the scene of lively trading and celebration. Architecturally, the Watrous house was a transition from Spanish colonial to territorial style. In the colonial period, rooms were multipurpose. In the Watrous home, there were parlors, bedrooms, and other special-purpose rooms. In Yankee fashion, fireplaces were in the middle of a wall rather than in the corner. Elaborate Greek revival mantelpieces framed an otherwise simple elliptical adobe hearth. The long exterior facade was graced by windows, shutters, and pedimented lintels similar to the officers' quarters at Fort Union, but the house plan conformed to the add-on construction of the colonial era.

Part of an old hacienda, the Sena Plaza in Santa Fe houses shops, galleries, and restaurants. The adobe building and courtyard are a good example of territorial style. The old wagon adds an element of rustic charm.

Tucson artist Chris Carson finished the adobe walls of his home in the Barrio district with dado detailing. He mixed pigments with the plaster to achieve a depth and glow that is impossible to get simply from a high gloss paint. The fireplace surround is a painted iron radiator, unearthed at a swap meet.

Territorial Update

The vocabulary that defines this home in Austin, Texas, combines architectural elements of the Southwest, Mediterranean, and regional vernacular, each of which is appropriate to the rough, hilly terrain that makes up the site. The house, designed by architect Heather McKinney, has a templelike shape, characteristic of territorial style.

The doors to the stair-tower entry were crafted from Ponderosa pine by an artisan in El Prado, New Mexico. The hardware was custom forged in San Antonio. The floors are paved in *saltillo* tile; the white oak stairs and railing were given a milk finish.

A long bar, actually the outer island of a pair in the kitchen, accommodates three stools for anyone who wants to sit and chat while food is being prepared. The marble-topped counter is fitted with a sink, and above it are floating glass shelves for glasses.

In spite of its traditional references, this home has a stripped-down appearance. Furnishings in the living room are contemporary, and the colors are neutral grays and browns, except for the patterned Oriental rug and the art work. The piece above the fireplace is mixed media and gold leaf, by Texas artist Michael Tracy.

The Territorial Revival

Despite the prevalence of territorial architecture during the Santa Fe Trail era, the railroad and the Victorian cultural baggage that came with it caused most New Mexicans to forget about frontier-style Greek revival architecture. In a dramatic renunciation of the style, the territorial *portal* on the Palace of the Governors in Santa Fe was removed in 1909 and "restored" with a Pueblo style interpretation. Fortunately, the same preservationist movement that redesigned the palace realized the value of other territorial buildings and preserved many of the city's nineteenth century homes.

The New Mexico capital in Santa Fe is a blend of territorial style with Greek revival and Pueblo architecture. Dedicated in 1966, the three-story circular building was modified to form the zia symbol, which is on the state flag. The roof is edged with brick coping, a typical territorial adaptation.

New Mexico has more than 300 sunny days each year, so this large sunroom, or glassed-in *portal,* gets a lot of use. The warm, bright space is just the place to eat a casual meal, grow plants, or gaze at the view of wide-open plains and distant hills.

Territorial Interiors

Because of its classical heritage, territorial interior design is refined and uncluttered. Its East Coast origins are expressed in furnishings from English and American colonial traditions that continue to give territorial rooms a direct link to the past. Chippendale chairs, a Georgian highboy, or a four-poster bed are spectacular accents alongside classic Navajo rugs, less refined frontier furnishings, and Pueblo pottery.

Color, proportion, and shape are important considerations in territorial rooms. Colors should be muted and cool. Gray, beige, ivory, burgundy, creamy yellow, and ocher dominate the palette, with brilliant turquoise, forest green, and vermilion highlights as trim paint and accessories. A territorial interior reflects a balance between two timeless looks: the organic colors and designs of the Southwest and the orderly perfection of the classical style.

A pie safe from Philadelphia holds a collection of vintage quilts.

The simplicity of territorial style has wide-ranging interpretations. In this delightful room, contemporary leather seating is teamed with warm pine tables and a primitive *equipale* chair. Color and pattern are introduced in a pastel dhurrie rug, pillows, and a subtle wallcovering sporting a diamond motif that often shows up in Native American art.

101

Territorial Ranch House

Architect Lawrence Speck drew from regional architecture and incorporated local materials into the design of this home in Burnet, Texas. Part of a 300-acre goat and cattle ranch, it also boasts a pecan orchard.

The double-height great room has 20-inch-thick walls made of cordoba creme, a local limestone. Adjacent to this part of the house, which also includes a dining area, is a two-story wing with a kitchen and entry on the first level and bedrooms above. There are enclosed porches on both levels, with a sleeping porch above. The third part of the house, on the opposite side of the living-dining area, is a master bedroom wing. A fourth segment is a mud room, where the family cleans up when they come in from the barn.

The grand-scale fireplace has a small firebox. Speck explains that not much heat is required in Texas. To keep it in scale, the opening is appropriately large. Blue tile makes the transition from the creamy stone. A window is tucked into one side of the chimney stack, creating an asymmetrical curiosity that adds architectural intrigue. The room is furnished with Victorian wing chairs that belonged to the homeowners' grandparents.

Southwest Victorians

*T*he year 1821 witnessed the dramatic opening of the Spanish Southwest to American settlers and adventurers, but the year 1848 saw the Southwest become the scene of one of history's largest mass migrations. On March 15, 1848, a San Francisco  newspaper printed a headline that would forever change the region: "Gold Mine Found." The golden city of Cibola, for which Coronado and other Spanish explorers had searched the Southwest, had been found. The California Gold Rush had begun.

The Bashford house in Prescott, Arizona, was built in 1877. A late-Victorian hodgepodge of styles, the house features a decorative truss with an Italianate window beneath it, beaded friezes over the windows, and Queen Anne spindles. When the house was moved about seven blocks, down a hill, to its present location in 1974, the whole town turned out to watch.

When Victorian home designs began to be imported into the Southwest from eastern cities, a variety of styles was often incorporated into a single home. The bay window in this home has multipanes above the bay, lacy fretwork in the front gable, and fancy-cut shingles on the surface. Its porch, although smaller than many of this era, boasts the ornamentation and spindles of Queen Anne style.

California Transformed

News of California gold reached Washington, D.C., in August 1848, and by early 1849 gold fever was an epidemic on the eastern seaboard. The sleepy Mexican port of Yerba Buena, was transformed in only two years into the thriving city of San Francisco, which is perhaps the greatest boomtown the world has ever seen. Between 1849 and 1852, the American population of California grew from 20,000 to 225,000.

In a quick-change process that was soon to be repeated throughout the West, San Francisco transformed itself rapidly and continually as thousands of fortune seekers were incorporated into the city. For a few weeks or months, the new arrivals lived in makeshift tent cities and shantytowns, but as soon as streets could be surveyed and wood-frame buildings constructed, they moved into more permanent houses. As the new arrivals made their fortunes, they built grander homes along more stately streets. There were occasional setbacks to the steady advance of progress. When it rained, streets became impassable quagmires and houses slipped off their flimsy foundations. Flash fires often wiped out entire city blocks of timber buildings, which were quickly rebuilt.

Such juxtapositions as a two-story red brick Italianate and a simple frame building with few details were found in many California boomtowns. This is Bodie, California.

This Queen Anne has all the defining characteristics of the style: a turret topped with a finial, gable detailing, fancy shingles to define the walls, and a frieze suspended from the porch ceiling. Built in 1897, the house is the birthplace of John Steinbeck.

The sometimes flamboyant style that is known as Painted Lady is taken to the limit in this San Francisco Victorian. Only five trim colors are used, but the effect is dizzying because of their combinations and serendipitous placement. Columns and corbels are different colors, as are capitals.

California Victorians

The latest American and European fashions of dress, entertainment, architecture, and home furnishings arrived daily in San Francisco Bay, overwhelming the Spanish and Native American influences on California home styles. For most of the nineteenth century, Americans tended to prefer the same building styles that were popular in England and the British Empire. Even though some uniquely American and European characteristics were incorporated into these styles, they are known as Victorian because the long reign of Queen Victoria of England corresponds to the period of their popularity. The Victorian styles include Italianate, Gothic revival, Second Empire, and Queen Anne.

Before the Civil War, the Italianate style was popular in eastern cities. Adapted from the architecture of northern Italian country houses, Italianate architecture features vertical

A San Francisco Victorian mansion decorated with continental elegance

proportions, heavy roof cornices ornamented with elaborate brackets, and decorative window hoods. As fortunes were won in California, substantial Italianate mansions and commercial buildings were built on the hillsides of San Francisco. Although many of these buildings were destroyed in the 1909 earthquake, the formality of Victorian architecture continues to shape the look of many San Francisco neighborhoods.

The rapid growth of San Francisco was not repeated in other western cities until later in the nineteenth century. The Civil War and continuing conflicts between the United States Army and Native Americans limited westward expansion until 1869. That year the last spike was driven for the first transcontinental railroad, uniting the Central Pacific and Union Pacific lines. On July 4, 1879, tracks of the Atchison, Topeka and Santa Fe Railroad were extended to Las Vegas, New Mexico, 26 miles southwest of Fort Union on the very soon to be defunct Santa Fe Trail.

Grant's General Building, Virginia City, Nevada

No matter what the exterior—Pueblo adobe or Southwest Victorian—interiors at the turn of the century were likely to have been influenced by the fashion of the day: lacy tablecloths; ornate fixtures, such as this brass and opalescent glass chandelier; and rich, gracefully proportioned dark-stained furniture.

The Sherman house in San Diego, California, was built in 1887. It is an example of a square-towered stick style, with its gabled roof and wooden wall cladding, interrupted by multiple patterns of decorated boards (sticks) raised from the wall surface for emphasis. There is a decorative king post's truss in the gabled roof over the third-level balcony.

The hipped roofs, turrets, and fancy porches and balconies of this Victorian home in Sacramento, California, are some of the broader architectural details prevalent in house styles at the turn of the century.

Victorians and Adobes

The railroad opened the Southwest to a range of cultural influences, many of which clashed with its complex culture that was based on centuries of exchange and tolerance among Native American, Hispanic, and Anglo residents. In some communities, such as Las Vegas and Albuquerque, there was immediate acceptance of the new architectural styles ushered in on the rails. In other towns, such as Santa Fe and Taos, the people were slow to adopt Yankee ways.

By 1880 many different Victorian building styles were in simultaneous use in America. Gothic revival was popular for churches and public buildings, and French Second Empire with its characteristic mansard roofs was favored for large homes. Queen Anne is a romantic evocation of English medieval cottages that is often embellished with wooden shingles cut in a variety of shapes. Leaded window panes, cut glass panels, and gorgeous stained glass windows flood Queen Anne interiors with a lovely interplay of colored and refracted light.

In Socorro, New Mexico, an early Spanish colonial town between El Paso and Albuquerque, Victorian homes began to supplant adobes during the 1880s, when a mining boom and the new railroad brought an influx of Americans to the area. The Lupe Torrez house, located next to the old San Miguel mission in Socorro, shows the blending of styles that became characteristic.

This home in Socorro is a modified adobe, with applied Italianate trim around the windows in the bay and fancy-cut shingles in the gable. The fluted columns have Corinthian capitals.

A red brick home in Socorro shows an eclectic blending of Queen Anne details in the porch and Italianate details in the bay window.

The corner beehive fireplace identifies the underlying Southwest architecture of this Victorian home.

Montezuma Castle in Las Vegas, New Mexico, designed by Chicago architect Daniel Burnham, is considered one of the finest examples of Queen Anne style in the Southwest. This balcony offers a 360-degree view.

The Queen Anne style offered a definitive contrast to the territorial style. Where territorial architecture is formal and symmetrical, Queen Anne buildings are delightfully complex, with oblique angles and shimmering facades. Territorial adobes hug the ground, presenting a stable profile, while Queen Anne houses soar skyward with unexpected shapes and angles. Two or more stories tall, Queen Anne homes express an interesting interplay of intersecting gables. With Queen Anne and the other Victorian styles coming to New Mexico all at once, traditional adobe construction had been nearly forgotten by 1895.

Freight trains imported a wealth of new building materials to the Southwest. The trains brought fired brick of many colors and styles, large panes of glass, shingles, cast-iron columns, pressed-metal ornamental window hoods and cornices, paints, wallpaper, pressed-metal ceilings, and hardwood flooring and paneling. Factory-made doors and window frames, milled lumber, porch columns, and moldings became available, and carpenter's tools and hardware made frame construction easier than ever before.

A large Queen Anne home in Las Vegas, New Mexico, shows the exuberance of Victorian style, with its variety of decorative materials, including shingles, stained glass, spindles, and barge board (the detail under the gable).

The floral patterns in the rug, chintz fabric, and fresh flowers give this Victorian sitting room a distinctly English flavor. The window seat, arched alcove, and some of the architectural details hint at the room's Southwest ancestry.

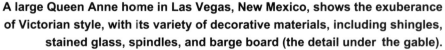

It is not only the wood-burning stove that gives this kitchen, in a Los Angeles Victorian, a nostalgic look. The absence of wall-hung cabinets, the stained glass fixture, the Oriental area rugs on the floor, and the Victorian fan ornamentation above the door create the kitchen's old-fashioned personality.

A fine example of frontier Queen Anne, this Victorian brick home in Socorro, New Mexico, was built between 1886 and 1900 by one of the town's leading residents. The ornamentation, particularly of the grand porch, is folk Victorian, with its turned spindle frieze and square porch supports that have chamfered corners.

Adobe interiors, as well as new construction, were transformed by crystal chandeliers, brass hardware, wool carpets, velvet and lace curtains, and walnut and oak furniture. The few homes with kitchens and bathrooms boasted porcelain bathtubs, washbasins, and toilets.

Some adobe houses were modified to look Victorian with the addition of porches made with manufactured columns, balusters, and trim. Victorian "gingerbread" adds special charm to an adobe home, with the wooden filigree in sharp contrast to the otherwise flat facade. Rural carpenters often used the milled house details they had seen in town as models for charming folk Victorian designs. The result is a picturesque blend of styles that has become a treasured New Mexico design motif.

The Hotel Beele in Kingman, Arizona, originally was built as an eating establishment in the early 1880s. It caught fire twice before the current structure was built in 1897. A 32-foot glass-enclosed atrium illuminates the lobby, which has a grand staircase and mezzanine. Navajo rugs hang from the walls. All the original furnishings and cabinets—even an old safe—are intact.

The Gilded Era

Between the arrival of the railroad and statehood (1912), many New Mexicans put aside their unique culture and attempted to take on American styles and values. The regular grid plans of Midwestern and Eastern cities became common in the Southwest, replacing or adjoining plaza-oriented Spanish colonial designs. In cities electric street lights and trolley cars became common. Brick and concrete sidewalks were built, streets were surveyed, new parks were built with neat, orderly rows of trees, and house lots were fenced in.

Many prosperous owners of adobe residences maintained their social status by "gilding" their houses with Victorian architectural details and furnishings. They planked over earthen floors and laid carpets, and stenciled their walls or wallpapered over the adobe. Carved wooden mantels were fitted onto the organic, sculptural adobe fireplaces. Factory-

The Herndon residence, a two-and-a-half story frame home in Prescott, Arizona, was built in 1893. Architectural features include a gabled and hipped roof, a six-sided pyramid that caps the corner turret, window bands in groups of two or three, and a rich assortment of wooden trims.

This delightful room in a California ranch house has a decidedly Victorian feel in its massing of furnishings and personal collections.

The barnlike, buttressed church of San Viconte de Paul in Punta de Agua, New Mexico, was constructed of adobe, but its tin roof is definitely Victorian.

made doors and double-hung windows were installed into enlarged openings cut into thick walls. Stamped-metal ceilings hid the *vigas* underneath.

Many preservationists and architectural historians may regret this compromising of adobe architecture with Victorian embellishments, but no one can deny the positive effect of the introduction of corrugated metal roofing. Heavy winter snows required the constant maintenance of mud roofs, which usually leaked no matter how much effort was put into them. By 1920 houses in the most remote mountain villages were protected from the elements by gable or hipped roofs clad in metal. Many adobe buildings, which might otherwise have been washed away, were preserved because of tin roofs.

Cozy sofas covered in chintz and wall-to-wall carpeting were some of the changes in interior design that proliferated during the Victorian Era.

A bedroom in the Bisbee Grand Hotel on Main Street in Bisbee, Arizona, shows the Victorian fondness for wallpaper, often combining different patterns. A brass-and-iron bed might have been typical of the original furnishings.

This tiny cottage in Prescott, Arizona, was built by H. William Stevens in 1907. It has a Palladian window in the center of the gable.

Boomtown Victorians Reborn

Victorian homes, storefronts, and county government buildings were built in boomtowns throughout the Southwest. By the end of World War II, much of this architecture had fallen into disrepair or been torn down. Small towns were deserted after the gold, silver, or oil had been extracted from the vicinity. Homes in farm and ranching communities were abandoned when the Dust Bowl and Depression forced people to move out. Victorian buildings in large towns and cities often encircled a crumbling central business district, and affluent families rejected them for new houses in new neighborhoods far from downtown.

Americans wholeheartedly rejected Victorian styles in the postwar years, preferring instead the international style, typified by suburban split-level and ranch houses. During the 1960s, urban-renewal projects razed inner-city and downtown neighborhoods, replacing Victorian architecture with parking lots, shopping malls, and housing projects.

This hip-roofed Victorian in Georgetown, Colorado, with its dormers, bay windows, and front porch, shows how well disparate styles can work together. Twentieth-century additions, such as the greenhouse, add to the delightful confusion.

Deep jewel tones—ruby, malachite, sapphire—were favorite colors for Victorian interiors, and designer Wayne Grant-Escano used this palette effectively in this bedroom. The woodwork is finished in a faux tortoise. A brass bed, art-glass lamp, Oriental rug, and paisley comforter add handsome touches to this masculine room.

The implicit ugliness of poorly executed international design prompted a few people to hold on to old neighborhoods and to restore the quality of life that is possible only in beautiful surroundings. Urban planner Jane Jacobs astutely observed a community's need for old buildings as early as 1961, commenting that "old ideas can sometimes use new buildings. New ideas must use old buildings."

In the West and Southwest, San Francisco and Santa Fe were the first cities to inspire historic preservation movements. In 1951 a group of San Francisco home furnishing designers and wholesalers bought several dilapidated buildings near Jackson Square and refurbished them. Their work captured the fancy of many more people, igniting a reappraisal of the Bay Area's historic buildings. In 1957 the citizens of Santa Fe created one of the nation's first historic districts in and around the Plaza. Their plan included stringent guidelines for authentic rehabilitation and compatible development.

Oil lamps, pots, and odds and ends hang from the tin ceiling of the O.K. Pearce Store in Pearce, Arizona.

The staircase in this Victorian home in Aspen, Colorado, is original, but the risers were removed to float the now carpeted stairs. The etched glass panels and brass hardware are new.

Some San Francisco streets are a textbook of Victorian architecture. The city has been a leader in rehabbing its turn-of-the-century buildings and in fostering the style known as Painted Lady, which calls attention to the marvelous diversity in styling through delineation with color.

The Worster Building, which is California mission style with its terra cotta tile roof, was added to Ghirardelli Square in 1964. The fountain, featuring bronze mermaids and frogs, was designed by Ruth Asawa.

Two dazzling San Francisco projects insured that the rediscovery of Victorian architecture would continue to build. William Roth spent $14 million in 1963 to transform the historic Ghirardelli chocolate factory into a shopper's paradise of boutiques, art galleries, restaurants, and courtyards. A $7.5 million facelift of the nearby Del Monte fruit plant, the Cannery, also joins brick and timber architecture with boutique shopping. Following the success of these two landmark developments, San Franciscans of many different economic backgrounds began to treasure and restore the city's Victorian row houses. Flower children and strict preservationists began painting the houses in complex and fascinating color schemes, based on personal preference, historic authenticity, or a combination of both. These houses became known as the Painted Ladies; they were an overnight sensation that is standing the test of time and serves to inspire Victorian preservations through the Southwest.

The red brick buildings at Ghirardelli Square date to the 1860s. The clock tower borrows heavily from colonial missions in California.

The red brick Ghirardelli Square in San Francisco is one of two major projects that pioneered the preservation boom in the Southwest. Named for the chocolate factory that once occupied the buildings, the square consists of 14 buildings on eight levels. The complex now houses more than 50 shops. The 15-foot-high illuminated sign dates to at least 1916. It went dark during World War II and was relighted in 1964.

After 1970 Victorian architecture became a status symbol for urban sophisticates and small-town architectural crusaders. As the design waves from the Bay Area rippled outward, entire communities and neighborhoods were transformed. Decaying houses and storefronts in Telluride and Crested Butte, Colorado; Las Vegas and Silver City, New Mexico; Bisbee and Prescott, Arizona; and Sonoma and Benicia, California, have now been restored to their former glory.

Investment in historic buildings was greatly encouraged by the Federal Tax Reform Act of 1982, which allowed a tax credit of up to 25 percent of a rehabilitation project's value. Though severely restricted by Congress in 1988, the Tax Reform Act attracted millions of dollars of new capital to rural communities across the country. Today, in many former boomtowns, exciting opportunities remain for prospective homeowners interested in historic property.

The interior of a San Francisco Victorian was gutted, creating a dramatic two-story living space that is furnished with streamlined leather seating and accented with a variety of ethnic textiles. A balcony maintains the open feeling on the second level, where the kitchen is located.

Eliminating small Victorian rooms to create a great room rehabbed this kitchen in a Victorian home in San Francisco. A spiral staircase becomes an architectural element. Other details are kept to a minimum. The cabinets are simple, with clean lines. Tile defines the kitchen; hardwood flooring is used in the living areas.

129

A collection of toys decorates the top of a mirrored wardrobe in this music room of a home in Angelino Heights, California. The furnishings are decidedly Victorian, including the Oriental rug and piano shawl.

The current interest in Victoriana has encouraged the development of a supportive home furnishing industry. Lumber mills now re-create wooden architectural components, such as cornices, columns, paneling, and balusters. Brass lighting fixtures and hardware are reproduced by many companies. Stained, beveled, and leaded glass windows are readily available. Victorian period furniture, carpets, textiles, and wallpaper are sold through many design stores.

A Southwest Victorian interior is likely to include such flourishes as a painted *trastero* or Navajo rug. Many home designers try to find antique furnishings, such as marble-top dressers, claw-foot dining tables, porcelain bathroom fixtures, beveled mirrors, wicker furniture, and worn rocking chairs. But quality reproductions of classic Victorian furniture designs are also available.

Southwest Victorian style is bold and innovative. The dramatic paint scheme of a home's exterior prepares us for extraordinary interior design. These houses are rarely conservative period interpretations, but they reflect an eclectic appreciation of Southwest culture. People who own Victorian houses are often collectors, and displays of antique dolls, maps, engravings, or Pueblo pottery may focus interior design on a particular theme.

In contrast to unadorned adobe walls, the surfaces of Victorian homes were papered or paneled. In this study dark wood paneling and shutters create a warm backdrop. Wall-to-wall carpeting continues the cozy feeling, while traditional furnishings add comfort.

Pueblo Revival

Spanish colonial architecture and its modern interpretations have a long history in the Southwest, but building styles based on the architecture of the Pueblo peoples trace their antecedents back several thousand years. The Anasazi were the ancestors of the modern Pueblo people and some of the first people to live in the Southwest. The Anasazi lived on the Colorado Plateau about 2,000 years ago. Their ancestors had been nomadic Basket Makers who lived in the desert.

In designing an adobe home in Carefree, Arizona, William Tull drew from such Moorish elements as an arched doorway. Flagstone paves the floor and a wool area rug anchors the seating. Asymmetry adds interest to the fireplace: On one side there is wood storage; on the other a *banco* provides additional seating.

The ruins in the distance are an eighteenth-century mission church. The kiva in the foreground suggests the dichotomy of cultures that exists in the Southwest. Poking out of the opening to the subterranean sanctuary is an asymmetrical ladder, a rustic form often embraced in today's interiors.

By around 300 A.D., the Anasazi had learned to grow corn, squash, and beans. Their homes were pits dug in the ground and roofed with logs, sticks, leaves, and mud. A central fire pit warmed and lit these lodgings. By 700 A.D. Anasazi potters were making pots of fired gray clay, decorated with black geometric designs and animal figures. More than 1,000 years ago, the Anasazi began to live in villages. Their houses were built by stacking flat stones to make walls that were held together with mud. The rooms were aboveground and were square or rectangular. The roofs of Anasazi houses were made by placing logs across the tops of walls. These beams were then covered with sticks, brush, and mud. Houses were linked together and rooms were stacked on top of each other. This kind of architecture is called a pueblo, from the Spanish word that means both village and people. While the people now lived aboveground, they continued to dig round rooms into the earth, but these enlarged pit houses, known as kivas, were places of worship where clans gathered to dance and chant.

The Anasazi built an interconnected network of a dozen major pueblos in Chaco Canyon, New Mexico. Pueblo Bonito is the largest structure there. Until the 1800s the 800-room pueblo, which stood five stories tall, was the world's largest apartment house.

Nestled beneath an enormous natural stone canopy, the Cliff Palace at Mesa Verde, Colorado, looks like a series of sophisticated sand castles. Its conical and square towers rise above low rectangular forms and large circles that are kivas.

During the thirteenth century, the Anasazi abandoned their rock palaces and established new villages in other parts of the Southwest. No one knows why the people abandoned their homes, but they stood silent for more than 500 years. In 1876 William Henry Jackson, a pioneering photographer, published photographs of the Anasazi cliff dwellings at Mesa Verde in southwestern Colorado. But the area was so remote that it was not fully explored nor properly protected from vandals until 1906, when the area was made a national park.

Once the Anasazi left the high plateaus, some of the people wandered into the highlands of the Rio Grande and settled near the river. Conditions in their new homeland forced them to change from building with rock to building with earth. The people living along the Rio Grande were colonized during the sixteenth century by Spanish invaders from Mexico and named the Pueblos. Other Anasazi settled in what is now northeastern Arizona; they are the Hopi. Another group migrated to northwestern New Mexico and became known as the Zuni. The three nations are related by blood, language, dress, architecture, and religious practices, but each developed distinct decorative styles, customs, and dances.

Two recurrent elements in the Southwest, the kiva ladder and chile *ristras,* decorate the facade of an adobe in Taos.

Elements traditional to Pueblo style join floor-to-ceiling windows to create an open but cozy living area in this Southwest home designed by Tom Ashe. The beehive fireplace, *latilla* ceiling, and cedar *vigas* define the room's historic roots, while the uncurtained view of rolling hills opens the style to a dramatic reinterpretation.

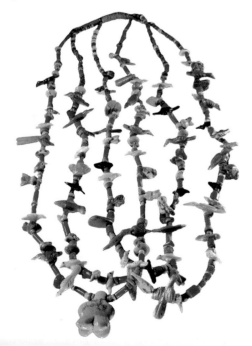

Taos has been inhabited continually for nearly ten centuries. When Spanish soldiers first saw the sunlit pueblo, they believed they had finally found one of the fabled Seven Cities of Gold. Sunsets still transform the dull clay buildings into luminous jewels.

From the family room and kitchen of a Santa Fe adobe, the outside view is a raised garden with a fire pit the homeowners call their kiva, framed by rounded and undulating walls. The terraces and steps are built with Arizona flagstone. Fetishes were painted on the back courtyard wall by local artists. The horse's head sculpture was carved with an axe. Spilling over the low courtyard wall behind it are blankets from nearby pueblos.

Wherever the people settled, they continued to build modular apartment houses, using layer upon layer of mud to create walls as tall as seven stories. Most rooms have only one entrance through a small door onto the central plaza of the pueblo or down a ladder through a smoke hole in the ceiling. The few windows are tiny, and floors are made of packed earth. Roofs continued to be mud-covered wooden structures, much like those built by the Anasazi. As the population grew, more pueblos were built and the space between the buildings became a plaza in which people gathered informally and for religious ceremonies.

This Santa Fe home was designed by the architectural firm McHugh Lloyd Tryk. The plan is open, with a fireplace dividing the living and dining areas. The fireplace retains the sculptural characteristics of adobe construction. The ceiling is a combination of rounded *vigas* and beams set off with white plaster. The interiors, by Arline Genis and Cheryl Genis Markham of Designers Circle Ltd. in Los Angeles, blend contemporary furnishings with the works of local artisans.

The Pueblo Revival of New Mexico

After the turn of the twentieth century, Spanish colonial revival architectural styles were extremely popular in California, Florida, and many parts of the Southwest. In New Mexico there also was a revival of the region's precolonial adobe architecture. The discovery of major Anasazi ruins at Mesa Verde and Chaco Canyon brought archaeologists into the area to explore the prehistoric culture of the Southwest. Researchers working in the new field of anthropology also converged on New Mexico to study the last intact remnants of Native American culture, the Pueblo nations. Reports of clear blue skies and incredible vistas soon attracted artists, photographers, and eventually writers and art patrons to Santa Fe and Taos, in particular. This cadre of East Coast intellectuals who fell in love with New Mexico has become known as the Santa Fe School. As a group they promoted a return to a distinctive and picturesque architectural style based on Pueblo architecture.

This swimming pavilion/spa includes an entertainment center, dressing and guest rooms, and a whirlpool. Architects McHugh Lloyd Tryk gave the solar-heated space plenty of windows, clerestories, and skylights. The murals were painted by several local artists.

When the Taos Gallery was built in 1960, architects took their cues from Pueblo and Pueblo Deco design. Familiar features include a stepped roof, anchored by a recessed band decorated with three triangles, and a horizontal row of ornamentation. The twisted posts were carved locally.

Santa Fe's Museum of Fine Arts is quintessential Pueblo revival style, with a courtyard orientation, wraparound *portal,* and projecting *vigas.* The building, designed by I.H. Rapp and built in 1917, synthesized a variety of architectural elements.

Rising in the distance beyond a gnarled tree is the Watchtower at the southern rim of the Grand Canyon. Built by architect Mary Colter in 1931, the structure is an amalgam of Pueblo masonry techniques with an Art Deco skyscraper. Colter's tower, a masterpiece of Pueblo Deco style, has a concrete foundation and a steel infrastructure.

Architect Mary Colter loved rough surfaces, asymmetry, and ornamentation. Even the handrails at the Watchtower were covered in rawhide. The blackened wall was painted in white with figures of animals and hunters. Hopi artist Fred Kabotie translated traditional myths and motifs with paint.

In 1909 the newly formed Archaeological Society decided to create a new museum to house the collection of the School of American Archaeology. The society remodeled the governor's palace on the Plaza in Santa Fe, which is the oldest government building in the United States. The territorial porch was removed, and the building was restored to its colonial appearance. This early restoration project and the museum focused public attention on the Pueblo revival movement.

Archaeological research in New Mexico had made more than a thousand years of Pueblo architecture accessible to architects and designers. With so many examples to use for reference, there were bound to be many different points of view concerning what was authentically and appropriately Pueblo revival architecture. Pueblo-influenced buildings at the University of New Mexico in Albuquerque and Mary Colter's Watchtower at the Grand Canyon were built before 1910. But the defining characteristics of the style were not firmly established until the Panama-California Exposition in San Diego in 1915.

Architect Tom Ashe applied a Pueblo idiom to this master bedroom-bath suite. A corner, raised-hearth fireplace is set into a stepped wall, which is echoed on the other side of the entry to the bath area. Teal-banded tilework, inset with a chevron design, surrounds the tub and decorates the shower; it is a characteristic Pueblo Deco ornamentation.

The simple black sphere was sculpted by Juan Hamilton, Georgia O'Keeffe's assistant and longtime companion. Its rounded form echoes the architectural shapes used in the entrance to the Saint Francis auditorium at the Museum of Fine Arts in Santa Fe.

The New Mexico pavilion for the exposition was designed by Isaac Hamilton Rapp and his brother William Morris Rapp. The Rapps' charming pavilion was a pastiche of the Pueblo mission facades of Laguna and Acoma, organized around a central courtyard. Massive roof beams and carved corbels, balconies, terraced walls, and the unique sculptural beauty of adobe captivated visitors at the exposition. By 1917 the pavilion had been adapted and reconstructed on the Santa Fe Plaza as the Museum of New Mexico's Fine Arts Building.

The museum was the first large-scale expression of Pueblo revival style, but Santa Fe architects soon began to interpret the style for homes. Mayan scholar Sylvanus Morley rebuilt and redesigned an old adobe an a hillside near the plaza in 1910. Artist/designer Carlos Vierra built a house in 1916 that was a fully realized Pueblo revival mansion. Vierra was so enthusiastic about this design style that he sold lots along Buena Vista Loma exclusively to builders who were planning to build "Santa Fe style cottages" on the property. Architects

Part of the charm of Pueblo architecture is the play with light that the sinuous curves and projecting *vigas* afford.

freely invented designs that included accurate details, such as fireplaces, ceilings, *bancos,* and niches. The simple linear house plans of the past and the formal symmetrical room arrangements of the territorial style gave way to houses designed for practical use and comfort. Blending the old and the new became a signature of the Pueblo revival style.

In 1912 Santa Fe's first city planning board was appointed. Its members set about renaming streets with Spanish names and recognizing certain buildings as historic sites. Many public buildings and houses were built in the Pueblo revival style. The Ancient City Movement in Santa Fe was a driving force throughout the 1920s. In 1920 La Fonda Hotel designed by Rapp and Rapp was built on the Plaza, and in 1922 the Pueblo style Federal Building in Santa Fe and the KiMo Theatre in Albuquerque were built. Art patron Mabel Dodge Luhan created a Pueblo revival house in Taos and gave D.H. Lawrence an adobe-and-log cabin nearby.

Even the door handles in the KiMo Theatre lobby are ornamental. The metal handles look like cookie-cutter kachinas hammered and incised to bring out their features.

The entry to a home designed by the architectural firm McHugh Lloyd Tryk features a clay fountain of a reclining woman pouring water into a vase. The walls, which have the look of aged adobe, are imbedded with small objects, such as shards, beads, and feathers. All are the work of artist Armond Lara.

The extraordinarily ornamental facade of the KiMo Theatre in Albuquerque was designed by Inez Westlake, who had a fondness for the shield motif, inspired by the Hopi artist Nampeyo. A band of shields alternates with elaborate spindles, setting off the third story windows of the tripartite facade.

A postcard of the KiMo Theatre in Albuquerque shows the building soon after it was built in 1927 by architects Robert and Carl Boller. The building is reinforced brick heavily stuccoed to resemble adobe plaster. Brilliantly colored friezes of Native American symbols grace the exterior, and the terra cotta ornamentation is ebullient.

This rehab of a ranch in Phoenix by architect Robert L. Nevins shows how Pueblo and contemporary styles merge. The ceilings were raised and several small rooms eliminated to create a more expansive space. A new set of clerestory windows and a window wall with doors opening to the swimming pool create a stunning indoor-outdoor relationship that reinforces Pueblo revival themes.

Pueblo Deco

After the 1925 Paris Exposition Internationale des Arts Décoratifs et Industriels Modernes, Art Deco, the sophisticated geometric style that the exposition originated, became an international design sensation. In the Southwest the strict geometry of Pueblo and Navajo art and architecture were quickly and easily blended with Art Deco themes to create a stylized variation of Pueblo style. The masterpiece of Pueblo Deco is the KiMo Theatre, a Route 66 landmark. The elaborate movie house has brilliantly colored friezes of Native American symbols on the exterior and terra-cotta cow skull sconces, carved and painted *vigas,* and wrought-iron railings shaped like rows of cranes in the lobby.

Buildings in the Pueblo Deco style were built throughout the Southwest. In Arizona, New Mexico, and Texas, the style was mostly confined to public buildings, such as hotels and county courthouses, but in California and Florida entire neighborhoods of Deco bungalows were built. The recent restoration of these neighborhoods is creating new interest in the clean lines and detailed ornamentation of the Pueblo Deco style. Bold tile-work designs; geometric motifs of animals, thunderbirds, and rain clouds; and pueblo profiles inspire postmodern designers throughout the Southwest.

Architect Adolf deRoy Mark gave the mantel in this Arizona house a unique Pueblo Deco interpretation, which blends perfectly with the high polish of synthetic granite tile flooring, stainless steel railings, and black leather Italian-designed chairs. Next to the fireplace is a sleeping niche. From the tiny window set into the wall, the homeowners can look out to Scottsdale.

Tile in the lobby of the KiMo Theatre

During the 1930s Miami Beach was a rapidly growing resort town. The demand for beach houses, hotels, and apartment complexes created an Art Deco building boom, which contributed hundreds of stucco variations to Pueblo Deco architecture. The style's free-flowing interior space, open-air balconies, and expansive windows complemented the Miami Beach lifestyle. Designers added a tropical panache to their work, with cast-concrete ornaments, friezes, and finials of stylized Florida fauna and flora. Instead of the pure white perfection associated with Pueblo Deco, Miami designers painted trim and accents in delicate shades of lavender, teal, salmon, peach, and moss green.

In contrast to the sometimes humorous, almost tacky, appeal of Pueblo Deco, young designers of Miami's Art Deco homes take a more serious approach, collecting authentic 1930s and 1940s furnishings. These include rattan furniture, floral pattern rugs, bedroom sets with wood veneer inlays, circular mirrors, and chrome lamps.

Cantilevered ledges were designed as sunscreens on the facade of the Carlyle Hotel in Miami Beach.

Candy colors distinguish many Miami Art Deco buildings. The Park Central Hotel shows some characteristic embellishments: A pair of decorative panels are covered with organic tendrils, and gridwork set into the facade creates another handsome pattern.

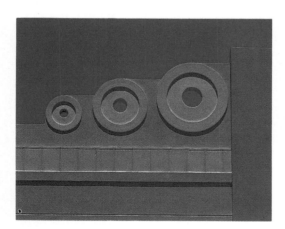

Graduating wheels at the roofline evoke portholes in a ship, a common Art Deco design element. The wheels are repeated on the other side of the Warsaw Building, which is sited on a corner in Miami.

Some Deco buildings were characterized by relief work to give them distinctive themes. Here at the Marlin, an apartment complex, the vertical patterns decorating the center of the facade are emblematic of the ocean, and the stylized design incised into the horizontal banding below the roofline suggests waves.

The west wing of the Zimmerman Library, originally the front of the building in Meem's 1938 plan

This room in the Zimmerman Library reflects John Gaw Meem's exquisite attention to details. Included are handmade tables and chairs with a strong Arts and Crafts influence, custom-designed metal sconces above the wainscoting, and mullion windows, some of which span 30 to 40 feet. Carvings on the ceiling beams represent Native American symbols and were made by craftsman from the San Juan and Taos pueblos.

John Gaw Meem

The work of architect John Gaw Meem has come to define Pueblo revival architecture more than the work of any other designer. Early proponents of the style, such as Sylvanus Morley and Carlos Vierra, took an archeological approach to their buildings, incorporating decorative details into their designs that were based on actual historical precedents. Their plans emphasized construction techniques and decorative detail. I.H. Rapp, the architect for the Fine Arts Museum and La Fonda Hotel, delighted in making a synthesis of eclectic details. His buildings feature an interplay of picturesque facades loosely based on mission churches. John Gaw Meem incorporated both the archaeological and the picturesque points of view and fused them with a skillful manipulation of massing and balance. Meem's architecture includes elements from Pueblo tradition and the mission revival style, as well as classical elements from the territorial style.

The Zimmerman Library, at the University of New Mexico in Albuquerque, was designed by architect John Gaw Meem, who brought together Pueblo, mission revival, and territorial styles. The 60,000-square-foot library opened in 1938.

The courtyard leading to an entrance of the Inn at Loretto includes a kiva fireplace.

A postcard shows the La Fonda Hotel in the 1930s. The original structure, designed by Rapp, Rapp & Hendrickson in 1920, melded Pueblo and Hispanic architectural styles. Fred Harvey acquired the hotel in the mid 1920s, and Mary Colter, distinguished for her mastery of Pueblo design, was hired to decorate the interior.

Farolitas, bags anchored by sand and illuminated with candles, line the rooftops of the Inn at Loretto in Santa Fe. The inn, designed by architect Harold Stewart, adheres to the design elements of Pueblo revival style.

In 1927 Meem designed an addition for La Fonda Hotel; his work on the hotel codified the Pueblo revival style, beginning what could be called the classic period of the style. Meem went on to employ Pueblo revival designs for residential, commercial, and institutional architecture in New Mexico. Toward the end of his career, Meem was instrumental in helping Santa Fe adopt the Historic Zoning Ordinance of 1957. The city's downtown core owes much of its aesthetic cohesion and integrity to this ordinance. In 1967 Meem's design for a *portal* for the plaza was built.

Meem and other architects working in the Pueblo revival style soon realized that adobe was costly and cumbersome for large-scale projects. Meem pioneered the adaptation of modern materials, such as concrete, steel, and hollow clay building tiles for Pueblo revival buildings. He also figured out how to make Pueblo buildings truly modern by incorporating electrical, plumbing, and heating systems into his designs. These innovations have allowed this style, with its roots deep in history, to continue to evolve throughout the twentieth century. The Inn of Loretto and the Eldorado Hotel, which were built during the last 20 years, show the viability of Pueblo revival architecture.

155

Santa Fe Design

The Juan Jose Prada home in Santa Fe, which was built in 1868, has been beautifully maintained. A corner fireplace, with one stepped side, divides a living area from the entry. Hanging from the chimney stack are Plains Indian pipe bags; on the ledge are tall Sioux moccasins (c. 1880) and a shorter pair of Zuni moccasins from the 1850s. On the stand is an Apache cap. The chairs and stool were painted by a Taos chief in 1920. A Germantown sampler (c. 1885) sits on the Mexican tile floor. A painted nineteenth-century Arizona cupboard holds a collection of kachinas. Just below the *vigas* hang a collection of Yei-bei-chai Navajo masks. On the floor is a Sumak rug.

An exposed wood wall shows early construction. The *banco* is made inviting with several pillows, upholstered in a Less Jofa print. A fringed Sioux saddle blanket is draped over an architectural block which also serves as a spot to display pots, one a Laguna (c. 1910) and the other a Hopi bowl (1925).

Adobe Charm

Ivy blankets a wall of a front garden of the Santa Fe home of gallery owner Nedra Mateucci. The tile set into the wall was designed by the internationally famous artist Diego Rivera in 1934. It shows a crowned shield, embellished with a warrior saint.

The enclosed gallery between the main and guest houses features a magnificent mural by Dorothy Stewart. Painted in 1935, the charming scene represents the interior of a second-class Mexican train; the mural was restored in 1950. Deep-well skylights flood the area with light.

The adobe charm of this lovely home can be fully appreciated in the guest house. The still-usable *horno* dates to the 1700s, but guests of this well-appointed household would never be expected to bake their own bread.

Pueblo and Pueblo Revival Interior Design

Viewed strictly from an architect's point of view, Anasazi and Pueblo interiors are perfect examples of the aesthetic known as organic minimalism. The living quarters of the ancients boasted no furniture, no wall hangings, and no ornamentation. The only design elements of these rooms were the architecture itself, the lovely ceiling *vigas,* and earth-surfaced walls and floors. The minimalist rooms of a pueblo were enhanced by beautifully made objects, primarily pottery and baskets crafted of organic materials and colors. Prehistoric Pueblo pottery is highly sophisticated and known for its abstract geometric inventiveness. In bare rooms pots and baskets resonate with unusual power. Photographs of Gerald Cassidy's house on Camino del Monte Sol show this purist approach to decor in a Pueblo revival home. Native American artifacts are carefully selected and placed for maximum effect. These minimalist rooms depend on expansive space, the integrity of adobe architecture, and highly charged objects to achieve their dramatic effect.

The marvelous sculptural quality of Pueblo adobe architecture gives this Taos bedroom its character. The corner fireplace features a curving *banco;* **its outer edges snake up a wall fit with** *nichos.* **Southwest art stands out against the crisp white background.**

A Mexican cart rests on the flagstone walkway to a Tucson adobe. The imbedding of the lintel, which caps an enclosed entry, is typical of the Pueblo style.

There is little need for furniture in this Tucson guest house. *Bancos,* **fitted with comfortable cushions and striped pillows, wrap around the fireplace. Folk art, along with the pair of pots that sit in illuminated** *nichos* **flanking the fireplace, make an arresting statement in an otherwise stark setting.**

Pueblo revival interiors are not necessarily minimalist. A mix of furniture, carpets, paintings, and Native American arts and crafts is found in many Santa Fe interiors. The Pueblo revival living room of archaeologist Sylvanus Morley and painter Randall Davey is a splendid example of this kind of interior decorating. In this well-known room, Pueblo pots are displayed among sturdy pieces of mission revival furniture. The house also incorporates a mixture of Navajo rugs, Hispanic antique furniture, American antique furniture, and Pueblo art. Pueblo revival interior design can also mix and match other Southwest design elements, including Apache baskets, Hopi kachina dolls, Navajo rugs, and contemporary Hispanic folk furniture.

Southwest Native American Crafts

To the untrained eye, Southwest Native American crafts might appear to be the work of a totally homogenous group of people. Once you become familiar with the work, you begin to see subtle but distinct differences in the pottery, weaving, jewelry, and other arts and crafts. In general Pueblos are best known for their pottery, jewelry, and kachina dolls; Navajos are famous for their weaving and silver work; and Apaches are renowned for their extraordinary baskets.

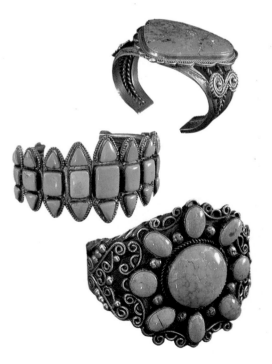

A sunken living room leads through French doors to a sleeping porch in this Cave Creek, Arizona, home. Architect Adolf deRoy Mark developed a strong Southwest theme with *saltillo* tile floor, a corner fireplace, and a beamed ceiling. The timbers used above the door are old ones from a mine near Santa Fe; some of them bear the carved initials of miners. In the sleeping porch, the architect designed brick columns with decorative capitals that were inspired by Anasazi ruins.

Pueblo Pottery

The Pueblo *olla,* or ceremonial pottery vessel, was first made in about 300 A.D. Each group of prehistoric Pueblo people had master potters who evolved distinctive regional styles. Anasazi black-and-white pottery displays dazzling geometric patterns, which are continually reinterpreted by contemporary potters. The Mimbres tribe of southwest New Mexico painted wonderfully stylized birds, animals, and humans on their vessels. These design motifs now appear on dishes and printed textiles.

Since 1880 potters in the western pueblos, Hopi, Zuni, Laguna, and Acoma, have developed pottery with both black-and-white motifs and polychrome (black, white, and red) painted designs. Zuni *ollas* sometimes show naturalistic deer and bears with red heart lines running through their bodies. Acoma and Laguna pots feature bold, flowery designs in polychrome, graced by scrolls and birds.

Pottery from Santa Clara is recognized by its highly polished black or red surface and carved relief designs. Potters at San Juan Pueblo pioneered the incising of fine, geometric patterns on reddish ware. At San Idelfonso a dynamic ceramics tradition revolves around the family of Maria Martinez and her husband Julian. They introduced matte black painted designs on gloss black vessels.

Nampeyo, a noted Tewa/Hopi potter, revived the tradition of polychrome Skikyatki pots. The jar and bowl in the front were crafted by Nampeyo; the jars top and left are by Fannie Nampeyo, one of her three daughters.

Although thoroughly contemporary in function, this Phoenix kitchen has many Pueblo references. Architect Robert Nevins kept the lines of the room geometric but left niches to display lovely pots to their best advantage.

Pot from San Idelfonso Pueblo

These are handsome reproductions of historic Mimbres pottery, characterized by crisp black-on-white drawings. Original pieces, referred to as "story bowls," were crafted during the twelfth to thirteenth centuries in southwestern New Mexico. The ceramic pots are distinguished by their elaborate geometric designs, which often are combined with mythical images of people, animals, birds, or fish.

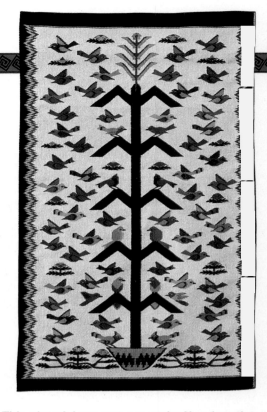

This pictorial rug was woven by Navajo artist Rena Mountain. It features 66 birds and other organic forms surrounding a central corn stalk planted in a ceremonial basket.

Navajos often weave figures into their rugs; this pattern is known as Blue Bird Dancers.

Navajo Weaving

Drifting down from the western plains of northern Canada six centuries ago, the Navajos gradually assimilated cultural traits from the Pueblos. They borrowed many ceremonial and religious practices and learned the craft of weaving. Over time Navajo weaving evolved from simple shapes to terraced zigzags and diamonds. The design of their blankets was heavily influenced by Mexican Saltillo textile design, which had been brought to New Mexico by the Spanish colonists.

By 1900 the Navajo economy was controlled by trading posts, such as those owned by Lorenzo Hubbell at Ganado and J.B. Moore at Crystal. The traders encouraged Navajo weavers to develop distinct regional styles of weaving, and a tremendous variety of styles developed during this century. Navajo weaving is collectible and likely to increase in value, but some old blankets are more valuable than others. Chief's blankets woven before 1900, the Ganado Red pattern pioneered by Hubbell, Crystal rugs, Two Gray Hills tapestries, storm-pattern rugs, pictorial rugs, and sand-painting designs are prized by collectors.

A dining room in a Santa Fe house designed by artist James Jereb is exuberant with saturated color. The eclectic furnishings give the space character. An antique fixture hangs over a pine table, with traditional armchairs upholstered with rather untraditional orange leather.

Navajo weaving from the early 1900s

Kachina Dolls

The Pueblos' rich spiritual and ceremonial traditions are reflected and personified by the kachinas. Each kachina has three aspects: It is a supernatural being that has particular powers; it is a ritual dancer, wearing a mask, body paint, and a costume that make him appear to be a deity, which is half human and half bird, animal, plant, or cloud; and it is a wooden doll that is given to little girls and babies. Kachina dolls introduce the child to the power of the kachinas and teach her the appropriate costume for each ritual dancer.

Hopi and Zuni kachina dolls are an important element of Southwest design. Old kachina dolls, especially those made for babies, are the most valuable. The best nontraditional kachina dolls are incredibly detailed and beautifully carved and painted. Popular legend claims that kachina dolls are blessed with a spirit that comes out at night to wander about the house, making it especially desirable to have at least one kachina doll standing on the mantel or coffee table.

Koshari, a clown kachina, provides comic relief during Hopi religious ceremonies.

At the Santa Fe Indian market, kachina dolls, both traditional and nontraditional, are admired and sold.

The taller white Quocha Hemis kachina and the shorter Hemis Mana, which represents the female, with large circles suggesting her hairdo, were crafted in the early part of the twentieth century.

The chimney to a Pueblo fireplace was sculpted as it tapers up to include a pair of ledges that simply delineate its form as well as provide display space for art. A *nicho,* marked by its own small lintel and positioned dead center above the fireplace opening, holds a Koshari, or clown kachina.

These shallow Apache baskets show a strong Yavapai influence.

Baskets

Long before they had learned to make pottery, the Anasazi made exquisite baskets. They coiled bowls, jugs, trays, and other containers in many sizes and shapes. Their technique, which bound coil weaving with splints, could make baskets that were woven so tightly they could hold water. The Anasazi even cooked in baskets, using hot rocks to heat water to cook dried beans. With the advent of clay pots, baskets began to be used exclusively as storage containers and did not need to be watertight.

When the Apaches and Navajos arrived in the Southwest, they developed their own basket-making traditions. The Hopis continue to weave colorful coiled plaques and baskets. The Papagos of southern Arizona, who are descendants of the Hohokam, also make excellent baskets, as do the Western Apaches of Arizona, the Jicarilla Apaches of northern New Mexico, and the Mescalero Apaches of southern New Mexico.

This Apache *olla* features geometric and life motifs in positive and negative styles. The figures in the black diamonds may represent coyotes; the other quadrupeds probably are deer.

A characteristic Pueblo built-in becomes a headboard set into a large recess. The ledges double as a display for a collection of baskets. A narrow set of shelves is built into the side walls of the bed.

Southwest Ranch Style

The American cowboy is the heir to the Spanish vaquero, *the Mexican* charro, *and the California* caballero, *who rode the range on swift Spanish ponies while the Southwest was a Spanish and Mexican colony. Hispanic cowboys developed most of the practical*  *clothing worn by all cowboys and many tools of the trade. Such well-known cowboy fashions as the wide-brim, tall-crown hat; mid-calf boots; spurs; and chaps were first used by*  *vaqueros. The Spanish bucka-roos, as the English called them, also developed the Western stock saddle, branding iron, and lariat.*

This home on the range in Jackson Hole, Wyoming, is furnished exuberantly in cowboy style, with Native American accents. The leather club chairs were designed by Thomas Molesworth, a designer from Cody, Wyoming, who created Western-frontier designs in the 1930s.

A log cabin in Colorado conjures romantic images of cowboys outfitted in fringed shirts, neckerchiefs, leather chaps, embroidered leather boots with fancy spurs, and wide-brim Stetsons, galloping through the sagebrush on horseback.

The Spanish colonists in the Southwest first introduced sheep, cattle, and horses to the region. Dry farming is a highly risky business, but herds of sheep and later cattle provided the early colonists with a dependable source of food. Cattle were first introduced into Texas in the 1690s, but the animals were only a small part of the area's economy until after 1865, when the railroad expanded the cattle market into northern cities. In California trading in cowhides played a significant role in the economy from 1820 to 1850.

The work of the cowboy was extremely difficult and not especially romantic. A group of ten cowboys usually managed a herd of 2,500 cattle. In the autumn they rounded up the cattle and branded new acquisitions to the herd. After watching over the cattle through the winter, the cowboys selected the animals that were ready for market and drove them to the nearest railroad yard, which was often hundreds of miles away.

This living room is anything but rugged. The room is a refined relative of every ranch-house living room with an orientation around the hearth. Pockmarked stone pots contrast with smooth carpeting and glazed terra-cotta tile. The scale is grand, with oversized ceramics, trees, and furnishings.

Brawny no-nonsense cowboy furniture is drawing a new generation of fans. This "scrub bench," designed by the W.A. Foster Co., is crafted of weathered wood, upholstered in steerhide, and decorated with handcast conchas.

174

By 1890 the broad plains of Texas had been fenced with barbed wire, and the era of the cowboy had passed into the romantic imagination of novelists, artists, showmen, and later movie makers. Artists Frederic Remington and Charles M. Russell, showman Buffalo Bill, and writer Louis L'Amour, among many others, helped shape the image of the cowboy as a rugged individualist. President Theodore Roosevelt, who felt that his life had been transformed by the years he spent on his South Dakota ranch, also championed the cowboy as an American archetype. In 1888 Remington illustrated Roosevelt's popular book *Ranch Life and the Hunting Trail,* and ten years later he painted Roosevelt leading the charge of the Rough Riders at San Juan Hill. Roosevelt recruited the Rough Riders from out-of-work and adventure-seeking Western horsemen. These men helped the future president win the Cowboys' War against Spain in Cuba.

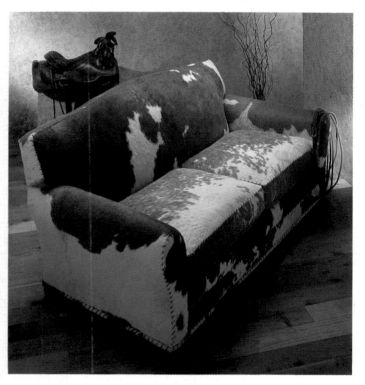

This sofa from the National Upholstering Company has a cowhide cover. The cushions and arms are detailed with handlacing.

The 7-D Ranch, just outside of Cody, Wyoming, is an ideal getaway. The sitting rooms ooze Western ambience. Molesworth-style furnishings sport decals with Western motifs; one lamp has a wagon-wheel base and a shade imprinted with a cowboy scene. These cowboy motifs are juxtaposed with traditional pottery, a Navajo rug, and drum tables. The river rock fireplace adds warmth, and the whisper of a flounce at the small pine-framed window conveys country charm.

During the twentieth century, cowboy culture has been kept alive by the motion picture industry. The first Westerns were silent films, starring such cowboy idols as William S. Hart and Tom Mix. Audiences had to imagine the sounds of gunshots, war cries, splintering chairs, fists smacking, and dialogue, but the genre captured the imagination of people everywhere in the world. A galaxy of cowboy stars followed in steady succession, including Hopalong Cassidy, Gene Autry, Roy Rogers and Dale Evans, John Wayne, and Ronald Reagan. Many other Hollywood stars have chosen to play cowboys when they got the chance. The ongoing proliferation of Western movies introduced the world to one of the most interesting Southwest styles. Known as ranch style since the 1920s, when the first dude ranches opened, this rugged blend of adobe, log, and stone construction can be decorated with everything from cowboy paraphernalia to choice English antiques.

Knotty pine paneling is common to Tucson ranches, like this one built in the 1940s.

An old cowboy worktable now serves for dining in this Comanche, Texas, home. The chairs are also old, with new rawhide seats. At one end of the table is a vintage pine bench; at the other a twig chair made by Texas artisans. Built by a local merchant in 1886, the limestone-walled house was vacant for 45 years before a recent one-year renovation.

Ranch Houses

Ranch style was shaped by the hard conditions on the prairies of the Southwest. Builders made use of whatever materials were available. Ranch houses in the mountains were built with logs; in places where trees were less plentiful, houses were built with adobe or stone. As the U.S. Army secured the region from attacks by Comanche, Apache, and Navajo raiding parties, ranch architecture moved away from fortified haciendas to loosely configured compounds of separate houses, barns, and outbuildings. Hip roofs covered with tin sheeting became common in the late-nineteenth century; earlier nearly flat sod or packed mud roofs topped log and stone as well as adobe houses. Ranch houses were furnished with a few hand-hewn chairs, a table, trunks, and perhaps a *trastero,* or cupboard. Buffalo, sheep, and other animal hides were laid on earthen floors at night to provide a place to sleep.

Architect Ron Mason built his Colorado log cabin along the Arkansas River, on the site of a gold mining claim called the Georgia Bar. Mason was inspired by early western log buildings and trips to Finland where he studied a technique called coping, which requires logs to be scribed to fit one another. Mason wanted his home to be environmentally sensitive, understated, and timeless. "The wonderful things about the cabin," he says, "is that it has a mountain ruggedness but also a very simple refined quality." Before the cabin was completed, Mason camped out; he still cooks out on the site, framed by river rocks.

181

Ron Mason built his cabin in three modules; each is about 18 feet long and 16 feet wide. The kitchen, which has simple pine cabinets and black plastic laminate counters, and living area occupy two full modules. The third module includes a loft area with a bedroom below. Furnishings are simple: a classic Alvar Aalto chair upholstered in leather, cylinder tables made from logs, and a sofa playfully draped with a zebra-patterned sheet. Mason designed the dining table with a glass top and natural base.

Many Spanish and Mexican colonial ranches were self-sufficient and had separate rooms or small outbuildings for a granary, a blacksmith's shop, a tannery, and a loom. Isolated ranches often had an *oratorio,* or a small chapel, where the rancher's family, servants, and *vaqueros* worshipped. For the altars of these shrines, woodcarvers fashioned *santos,* polychrome wooden statues of saints. Today an antique or modern *santo* can be the focal point of any style of Southwest room.

After the Civil War, as more and more pioneers from the United States arrived in the Southwest, and cattle ranching expanded in eastern New Mexico and West Texas, an American ranch style developed. The refined Victorian style that was popular in urban centers did not translate well into the harsh reality of the plains, although some elements of Victorian design could be found in many Southwest ranch houses. Ranch style was rough and rustic; buildings were simple and sturdy, with massive stone fireplaces, plank floors and walls, and raftered ceilings. A shaded *portal* welcomed hot dusty cowboys with a mix of unmatched chairs.

The beautiful views don't quit in the loft bedroom, which has a drafting table positioned in front of the windows for inspiration.

Log houses have a surprising range of exterior and interior effects, created by their builders' choices to strip logs or leave on the bark, or to square off the logs or leave them round. In the Southwest logs are often combined with adobe, plaster, stone, or milled lumber to create endless variations on this straightforward theme. In places where timber was scarce, stone houses and barns were built, with and without mortar. For greater protection against the weather, some stone buildings were covered in adobe. In Texas pink and white limestone is treasured for walls and fireplaces. New Mexicans used the available sandstone, also called flagstone or ledgestone, to build houses, stables, and storage buildings. (Some of these buildings are still standing in Pecos River valley villages, such as San Jose and Villanueva.) At higher elevations rounded river rocks and mountain stones are combined with logs to fashion cozy ranch houses or cottages for dude ranches.

Sleeping in this cedar-post bed made by Hill Country Texans may impart the feeling of being one with nature. The pillows are covered with collectible Beacon blankets. Their patterns complement a collection of Navajo blankets folded over the footboard. Above the bed is a panoramic photo of a 1926 Oklahoma rodeo.

In spite of rustic log-and-stone walls, this dining room takes a dressed-up approach to Southwest style. It is not quite the tux-and-cowboy-boots approach to design, but this collection from Thomasville is a lot more sophisticated than the usual ranch house interior.

184

The architecture of this New Jersey condominium is contemporary, but the homeowner has an affinity for the Southwest. She adapted her love of the region to the setting. A pair of black pine love seats are upholstered in cowhide. A contemporary rug is patterned like a Navajo geometric. A kiva ladder leads to a loft.

Ranch Style

Decorating a rustic ranch house requires wit, an eclectic sense of style, and a passion for nostalgia and Western pop culture. The cowboy style's recent resurgence in popularity gives designers a wide range of furnishings and accessories that look just right in a ranch house. Southwest ranch houses have always displayed locally made arts and crafts, including Navajo rugs, Pueblo pottery, Spanish colonial furniture, and Hispanic and Mexican crafts. Now, as in the past, a ranch house is home to just about everything anyone brings inside. The defining characteristic of this style is rugged comfort, and with that almost anything goes.

At the turn of the century, Americans did not hesitate to furnish their ranch houses with the most sophisticated furniture they could afford. Treasures arriving by the railroad

This award-winning Navajo rug, woven by Stella Todacheeny of Greacewood, Arizona, is one of the finest examples of the Ganado style. The wool was handspun and the colors are natural, except for the red and black that have been aniline dyed.

A vividly patterned new Pendleton blanket is the dramatic cover for a highly carved club chair from the 1940s. Pendleton blankets were first made around 1896 in Pendleton, Oregon. Even then, they had multiple uses: People slept in them, wore them, and bartered them.

The crowning glory of this horn lamp is a shade sewn from a Beacon blanket, made in about 1930. The creator of this lamp, a former New York stage designer, dyed fringe to match the blanket and lined the shade in vintage fabric.

The base for this pine lamp brings together two strong symbols: a saguaro cactus and a cowboy figure on a rearing horse. Designed by Duncan Reed for his company Reed Bros., the lamp is both whimsical and evocative of the romance of the Old West.

included marble-topped dressers and vanities, kitchen sideboards, and four-poster beds. These showy new pieces took their places alongside handcrafted quilts and punched-tin pie safes. A simple Texas ranch house might boast an elaborate Victorian hall tree in the Eastlake style next to a unique hatrack crafted of polished cow horns. Lamp stands, chairs, mirrors, and chandeliers also were made from horns and antlers. Chairs were either fancy, factory-produced versions of any Victorian style or simple home-built straight-back designs. Great dining tables of pine and mesquite, preferably worn, nicked, and proudly displaying knots, burls, and prominent graining, are the cherished heirlooms of many Texas families.

Manufactured furniture, especially wicker pieces, was popular on ranches during the early twentieth century. By the 1930s major furniture manufacturers had begun to introduce distinctive Western styles, including California-inspired Monterey lines, brightly painted Mexican "Fiesta" furniture, and the wagon wheel style, which decorated many motel rooms along Route 66 and many little boys' bedrooms. These examples of cowboy kitsch are now highly collectible, and along with mission and Taos furniture, they complement any ranch interior.

A trio of club chairs from the 1940s get verve with coverings of Beacon camp blankets, which are about the same age as the chairs. The designs exude oomph and personality, offering an invitation to come and sit by the fire.

This "High Country" bed is part of the Naturalist Company's "American Frontier" collection. It is handcrafted of oak and trimmed with buckskin lacings. The log end table and twig lamp have a strong Southwest spirit. On the bed is a trader blanket; over the foot is an all-wool saddle blanket.

The lines of this saddle-arm bench designed by the National Upholstering Company are flattered with the color and geometry of a blanket by Ralph Lauren.

During the cowboy craze of the thirties, a Wyoming designer, Thomas Molesworth, along with other furniture designers, created sophisticated ranch furniture. Molesworth's approach was eclectic but original. Using his trademark knotty pine for furniture frames, table legs, and lamp stands, Molesworth produced a luxurious look using authentic Chimayo (New Mexico) Hispanic weaving for upholstery. Molesworth was a master of theatrical effects, as is clearly demonstrated by his chandeliers, where cut-out, wrought-iron silhouette scenes of frontier life, such as buffalo hunts, glow magically from a hidden light source.

Rustic cowboy style, employing whatever was available on the prairie, has inspired several popular designs. An enterprising ranch hand probably invented the cowhide chair by lashing a hide to four sawed-off branches. Today variations on this design range from hide-and-cedar Mexican equipale chairs to leather-and-walnut reclining chairs with matching ottomans. Besides being a chic upholstery material, cowhide (especially white with black or brown spots) is a fashion statement for well-heeled urban cowboys and cowgirls. Cowhide patterns are found on bed linens, shower curtains, throw rugs, lamp shades, bowls, trays, salt shakers, and just about everywhere else.

This saddle-stitched leather chair boasts down-filled cushions, a fringed skirt, and pillows.

Southwest artifacts become art objects when they are hung on a craggy limestone wall. A deer head, unusually shaped gourds, dried herbs, Indian corn, and antique wooden cooking utensils decorate this wall in the kitchen of a home built in the 1870s by Alsatian settlers near Castroville, Texas.

The library at the 7-D Ranch is brimming with artifacts from the Southwest.

Everyday meals take on a Southwest accent in this contemporary kitchen, with *saltillo* tiles on the floor; a Mexican *equipale* table and chairs, made of pigskin and split cedar; and a table setting of Navajo-patterned place mats, black and turquoise stoneware, Italian serving bowls, and the heavy green stemware from Mexico.

This contemporary log home in Colorado has a distinctive Southwest flair. Sitting at the edge of a loft is an old Mexican bench, and flung over the top railing is a collection of Pendleton blankets and old chaps. A horn side chair is covered with an unexpected floral print. The rug's pattern reinforces the blankets' geometric motifs.

Much Southwest country furniture is made of willow or pine, as it has been for decades. Bent willow chairs, tables, and bed frames are similar in design to Adirondack camp furniture. Dyed and painted willow twigs used as inserts and accents give the Sombraje collection of Santa Fe a uniquely Southwest look. The best-known material for ranch furniture is stripped pine logs that are sanded smooth and made into elegant four-poster beds and sturdy legs for dining and accent tables, sofas, easy chairs, and armoires.

Another major element of Southwest ranch style is Pendleton wool blankets. Woven in gorgeous multicolored designs since 1900, Pendletons were once used primarily as shawls by Navajo women and bed coverings by everyone else. Within the past few years, such major designers as Ralph Lauren have integrated the Pendleton look into furniture upholstery and winter jackets. Pendleton sofa pillows and throws complement any ranch interior.

In some nineteenth-century ranch houses, cowboys burned their brands into the wood paneling, nailed a horseshoe above the door for luck, or hung the tools of their trade over pegs in the walls. Today horseshoes, cattle brands, leather tack, and anything made of wrought iron are popular additions to any ranch-style home. Horseshoes are made into bookends, coat racks, potholders, or garden ornaments. Plank walls, doors, and tables are branded for an authentic Western look. Stamped floral-pattern leather work, which originated in the Southwest, is now a popular treatment for everything from saddles to sofas.

Cow skulls, deer antlers, and small animal skins decorate many ranch houses. Celebrated by Georgia O'Keeffe in her New Mexico paintings, the cow skull has recently conquered America's design centers. Bleached, painted, or made up with turquoise, feathers, and other power symbols, designer cow skulls are now almost an art form, with roots in the decorated buffalo skulls made by many Plains Indians.

This loft bedroom was designed for children. A pair of trundle beds provide storage beneath. Skylights illuminate the space for daytime playing and allow the children to gaze upon the stars at night. A playful cow's head decorates the wall, and the moo-theme is continued in the bed linens.

The architectural firm of Ford, Powell and Carson was called on to design several additions to a 1930s cottage in Kerrville, Texas. This great room is anchored by a towering central fireplace made from the same stone used in the original house. The design is highly symmetrical, with a pair of passageways flanking the fireplace and the arrangement of two large couches and a table, as well as porches on each side. The interior was kept light, with special attention to the woods used. The cedar ceiling and walls were stained in a honey shade; the mesquite used for the floors was bleached.

In designing this home in Arroyo Hondo, Santa Fe architect Beverly Spears set out to create a contemporary expression of traditional adobe architecture. Her plan included a gabled roof, with beams made from vintage wood, and an open living space. The floors are polished concrete, with a pine inset that visually warms the central space. The living space teams a Morris chair with a traditional rolled-arm sofa and an old pine table. The iron chandelier over the dining table was crafted by Santa Fe artisan Tom Joyce.

California architect Alexander Seidel drew on Southwest rural architecture, with its simple forms and rustic materials, to fashion this seven-level home in Walnut Creek. The exterior is stucco with a copper roof, and the interior walls are plaster. The beamed ceilings were crafted of pine and spruce. A *nicho* over the lintel holds a decorative pot. The homeowner, an artist, painted the dining room chairs herself.

The ranch house kitchen is a warm, welcoming place where you can expect to be served a bowl of red chiles and *frijoles.* Hearty meals that recall chuck-wagon fare are cooked on wood-burning cast-iron stoves with a heavy cast-iron skillet and a baked-porcelain coffee pot. Fiesta ware or other Western-motif dishes add zip to even the hottest chili. There is an amazing variety of collectible and contemporary cowboy kitchen gear, including cow salt and pepper shakers, boot toothpick holders, and mini branding irons to burn into steaks, that capture the spirit of the campfire.

A new breed of Southwest furniture designers is producing sophisticated, striking, and sometimes corny art pieces. L.D. Burke III of Santa Fe crafts Texas-sized chairs and sofas out of hand-hewn wood and leather cushions. Burke adds cow horns and painted hoofs to complete his ranch theme. Burke's complete line includes spin-offs inspired by Thomas Molesworth, featuring antler-winged desks and frontier-scene silhouettes. Burke freely incorporates such cowboy

The muted tones chosen for this kitchen reflect the colors of the earth, which influence building styles throughout the Southwest. The cabinets have traditional detailing on their paneled fronts; the *saltillo* floor tiles, *equipale* chairs and table, and such accents as area rugs, pottery, and a cactus give the room Southwest accents.

Architect Robert Peterson enjoyed the task of renovating a turn-of-the-century building on a 700-acre ranch just above the Napa Valley. This kitchen was once a post office. The wood frame exterior wall was attached to the end of a stone building. The plaster wall is almost two-feet thick. The wood frame casement windows, dressed with sheer cafe curtains, are original. A local carpenter built the cabinets and towel bars. This simple galley kitchen has a lot of rustic charm.

Handforged horse tether, Vail, Arizona

The appeal of this interior, designed by Sharon Grady of Design West in Aspen, is its use of contrasts. The sofa upholstery is a neutral, textured fabric; opposite are a pair of overstuffed leather chairs, with blankets slung casually over their backs. A lodge-pole table with a glass top sits on an Oriental rug. A Remington bronze on the table and a tall cactus go with the territory. The plastered fireplace, which has the look of adobe, is set on a window wall and makes a dramatic silhouette in the sunlight.

equipment as rifles and spurs into his furniture. In another Santa Fe studio, cowboy style joins Art Deco to become Cowbeaux, a new line of furniture designed by Wayne Buckner. Cowhide and even faux leopard designs are married to streamlined Deco chairs and tables. Taos designers Andrea and James Rannefeld paint cowboy silhouettes and other Western motifs on traditional New Mexican colonial furniture, such as *trasteros,* in their Cowboy Country Collection.

Unlike the earthy ranch interiors of the 1890s, today's Southwest ranch interiors display a heady blend of opulence, nostalgia, and exuberance. Some of the country's finest designers have reconsidered cowboy style to come up with this pleasing mix. With a palette of natural woods, cowhide, leather, tin, Pendleton and Navajo blankets, bone, horn, and wrought iron, Southwest ranch style is as much at home in any house as it is at home on the range.

Architect Lawrence Speck designed this home in Austin, Texas, to take advantage of beautiful views to the hills and beyond. The ranch house is a series of long slender rooms, some of which step out onto porches. Buried inside of the extra-thick stucco walls are air-conditioning ducts and wiring. The living room embodies a rugged warmth, with a pine ceiling, stepped stone fireplace, and *saltillo* pavers on the floor.

Splashes of the Southwest

The striking dining room set combines an old Mexican table with straw-seated Spanish chairs. A New England apple tray cleverly decorates the table. The Southwest cabinet may have been intended for pie storage at the turn of the century; now it houses Pendleton and Beacon blankets. For a finishing touch, colorful baskets from the mid 1800s adorn the top of the cabinet.

The details of the living room are eye-catching. The blanket rug is new, but the dress on the wall is Navajo (c. 1850). Charming touches are the miniature Adirondack chair on the coffee table, the hanging fishing creel, and the Mountie hat.

The handmade four-poster bed was lovingly planed by a Pennsylvania Dutch craftsman in the late 1700s. The quilt is an antique; the rug is Navajo. For a hint of something different, a hat box and an old Stetson from the 1920s get a place of honor atop a side table. A utilitarian New England pie storage cabinet serves as a nightstand. The old dolls provide a nice finishing touch.

Modern Design in the Southwest

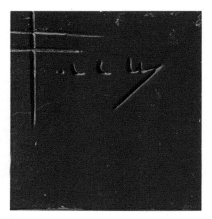

Before the international style became the dominant theme of twentieth century architecture, many American architects focused on distinctive re-

gional design elements in their work. Few of them withstood the onslaught of new ideas imported from Europe after World War I. Frank Lloyd Wright, whose work is distinctly American, was just about the country's only major architect who maintained and continued to develop his own unique architectural vocabulary. Wright developed a significant part of this vocabulary by observing the landscapes and indigenous architecture of the Southwest.

Frank Lloyd Wright used red volcanic stones from the site and poured them into concrete to create the desert masonry walls at Taliesen West, the architect's Scottsdale residence and studio. This bell tower sits over the kitchen and holds four bells salvaged by Wright from churches.

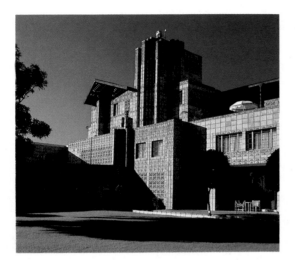

The Arizona Biltmore Hotel in Phoenix was completed in 1929. The building's design, with its irregular masses, deep shadows, and modulated light created by patterned sandstone bricks, reflects Wright's concept of "harmonizing the building with the terrain."

While his influence on modern architecture in the region was almost nonexistent, Wright is an important influence on post-modern Southwest architects and on many Pueblo modern designs.

Most of Wright's buildings were designed to fit their sites, aesthetically adapting to the terrain and structurally conforming to its particular characteristics and demands. Until he was commissioned to design the Imperial Hotel in Tokyo in 1914, Wright worked primarily in the Midwest and occasionally on the East Coast. While he was completing the hotel, Aline Barnsdall offered him a commission to build a large house on Olive Hill in Los Angeles, which he completed in 1920. Since Spanish colonial architecture was the quintessential California style of that time, Wright might have been expected to reinterpret mission architecture in his own way. Instead he went further back in time to interpret Mayan architectural motifs in poured concrete. Hollyhock House was the first home in America built with this material. The thick concrete walls keep the house cool on sunny days. The house takes its name from Aline Barnsdall's favorite flower, which was sculptured abstractly into the concrete walls.

Richly embellished textile blocks create light-and-shadow play on the facade of the Arizona Biltmore. Hopi sculptor Emry Kopta helped translate the pattern to stone.

The circular Aztec Room of the Arizona Biltmore suggests a kiva, with its somewhat flattened ceiling and ribbed supports.

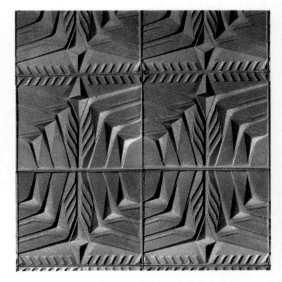

Block detail, Arizona Biltmore

Architect Will Bruder describes this Cave Creek, Arizona, home as "contemporary desert country." He oriented the architecture to frame views of the desert between piers of stone.

This Albuquerque house is an heir of Wright's Southwest style. Architect Berent Groth designed a contemporary structure with a Southwest character, and his building materials included masonry, wood, and glass. A *portal* defines the east side and is set off dramatically by a pair of cottonwood trees.

The house Wright built for Alice Millard in Pasadena in 1924 is made of concrete block, which at the time was considered an inappropriate material for home construction. In his design Wright treats each block as part of a giant tapestry, giving each an impressed design that forms part of a larger pattern when it is built into a wall or pier. The motif of La Miniatura is the eucalyptus leaf. The house, which was built in a shady ravine, was well received and other California commissions for cement-block houses followed.

In the winter of 1927, Wright visited Arizona for the first time. He built a desert camp in the San Tan Mountains near Phoenix, called Ocotillo, which is the name of a desert plant. The camp was made entirely of wood and canvas. The series of structures was arranged in abstract geometric compositions. Wright and a team of 15 draftsmen used the camp while they worked on San Marcos on the Desert, a resort hotel near Chandler, Arizona, which was never completed.

The Norman Lykes residence in Phoenix, constructed between 1966 and 1968, was designed by Frank Lloyd Wright. All the elements of the plan are circular segments. The building is constructed of desert-rose concrete block and Philippine mahogany.

A solid masonry halfwall displays art. It separates the entry from a breakfast area. The corridor leads to the *portal.* Designer Berent Groth had the fir ceiling and woodwork varnished to give them an eye-catching sheen.

In 1938 Wright returned to Arizona and bought land in the desert northeast of Phoenix. On the gradually sloping site against the foothills of the McDowell Mountains, Wright built Taliesin West, the winter residence and workshops of his architecture school, Taliesin Fellowship. During the summer months, the architecture students in the fellowship lived and worked at Taliesin East in southwest Wisconsin. For Taliesin West the architect designed a building with terraces, broad steps between levels, and a triangular extension, all of which echoed and expressed the mountains. Indigenous volcanic rock and huge redwood beams, with canvas panels between them, continued the desert themes.

This stunning gray-and-turquoise color scheme was part of Frank Lloyd Wright's 1950 design for the home of *Arizona Highways* editor Raymond Carlson. Recently architect Charles Schiffner faithfully restored the Phoenix house.

During the restoration the patio slabs were stripped and stained the original muted red shade that Wright had specified. Phoenix landscaper Adam Child trimmed the trees and installed new plantings to complement the architecture. Wright's tremendous attention to detail is evident in the cube, which is fitted for night lighting.

Wright designed the home on a grid system. Sweeping horizontal lines connect the house with the earth and diminish the height of the three-story stack at one end. Hot-pink butterfly chairs and 30 plastic flamingos add a whimsical counterpoint to the no-nonsense design.

Wright designed a new Arizona state capitol in 1957, but it was never built. The buildings Wright designed for Arizona State University a few weeks before his death in 1959 were the first public buildings of his design to be built in Arizona. While these buildings do not immediately recall architectural forms associated with the Southwest, Wright's adobe Pottery House is highly respectful of indigenous Pueblo architecture without aping its forms. The house was designed in 1941 but was not built until 1985. The bowl-shaped house sits in the foothills overlooking Santa Fe through uniquely shaped windows, some of which follow the house's contours while others resemble eyes.

The original owner used this top-level bedroom as a study. The awning windows open, and Wright carefully calculated the views to direct the eye over the rooftops of the nearby neighbors' homes.

Frank Lloyd Wright continued the exterior grid in the living room of this Phoenix house. Full-length windows face north onto the garden; the opening at the end of the living room leads to a small sitting area, created when the carport was enclosed in the 1970s. The tables and hassocks are reproductions of Wright originals that were in the home. The armchairs and lamps are interpretations of Wright's designs by Phoenix architect Charles Schiffner.

211

The owner of this Grand Junction, Colorado, home worked as an archaeologist in New Mexico before she became a physician. At her request architect Ed Chamberlin modeled the floor plan after Pueblo Bonito in Chaco Canyon. A crew of Navajo masons who restore ruins laid the sandstone.

Modern Architecture in the Southwest

While Frank Lloyd Wright's work in the Southwest fitted the land and often spoke directly of its history, his work is not typical of modern architecture in the region. The international style was imposed on the Southwest in much the same way it was foisted on the rest of the United States. The slick, clean lines of the style had been developed to suit the need for quickly built, inexpensive housing for workers, who immediately and universally rejected the impersonal housing blocks built for them. The cause of international style was then taken up by several prominent American architecture schools that encouraged their wealthy corporate patrons to build glass office towers in Phoenix, Houston, Miami, and Los Angeles, as well as Manhattan, Bonn, and London.

Architect Ed Chamberlin was influenced by Pueblo kiva design in planning this living room. Following the original plan of Pueblo Bonito's middle kiva, he felt a round sitting area was appropriate and designed the seating to fit the space.

The flagstone-paved entrance to this Grand Junction home features a door handcarved with a sun motif. The stairs accentuate the kiva shape. The treads are carpeted, the risers tiled. A collection of pots and black-and-white photographs make a striking display.

Wright himself invited the first proponents of international style to California, when he recruited Rudolf Schindler, a Viennese architect, to supervise his Los Angeles office. Schindler asked his friend Richard Neutra (also a Viennese architect) to join him, and by 1927 each architect had designed a house for Dr. Philip Lovell, a well-known health book author. These houses were among the first residences in America to be designed in the international style, which originated in Germany at the end of the World War I and dominated American architecture until the 1980s.

After World War II, many cities in the Southwest were reshaped with slick glass cubes, which mirrored the clear blue skies but were otherwise without distinguishing characteristics. School buildings that might as well have been factories or shopping malls and neighborhoods of almost identical houses were built in the deserts and ranch land

Huge cottonwoods tower above this Colorado home that was modeled after Pueblo Bonito. Although the building is only two stories tall, the horizontal scale of the windows and the pitch of the roof give it scale.

French doors lead out to a flagstone-paved courtyard. The oak cabinets were designed by architect Ed Chamberlin. Upper and lower cabinets are tucked into the curved stone wall. Above the buffet are three shelves for display. The homeowners purchased the handcarved mahogany chairs and tables from a used furniture store in southwest Colorado. They were the gift of Yucatan craftsmen to a doctor who worked in their village.

A view to the courtyard shows a cedar pergola, planted with ivy and other plants. The freestanding wood stove up the stairs is nickel plated. A second level, up another half flight, leads to three bedrooms and a bath.

Sited on a rocky promontory, this Albuquerque home grew out of a response to the spirit and culture of New Mexico as well as to its rugged terrain. The house, says architect Glade Sperry, was designed to look as though it was part of the geology of the site.

around these modern cities, while older downtown neighborhoods were virtually abandoned. Oil and cattle barons and new Sunbelt industrialists chose slick modern architecture because it was the architecture of choice for other successfully managed international businesses. While an oil cartel may feel at home in a big glass cube, people living in international-style public housing in Los Angeles, Phoenix, Houston, and other Southwest cities found themselves in the untenable position of having to make high-rise concrete boxes habitable. The global and ultimately unsuccessful application of a single architecture style to so many different kinds of projects has led many people to rethink the principles of international style.

Most architecture schools embraced the international style, but when asked to design private homes, many architects compromised the aesthetic to please their clients. The ranch-style house that was developed in California after World War II is one such compromise. Architects borrowed elements from familiar Spanish colonial architecture and came up with low-lying houses sprawling horizontally across their lots with deep, shaded porches that recall *portales.*

The contemporary attitude of this living room, in an Albuquerque home designed by Glade Sperry and Cindy Terry, has several important Southwest references.

The landscape of the Sandia Mountains is a primary design element in this room. Glass doors lead to an outdoor dining patio with its own fireplace, further expanding the vistas.

Turtle by Helen Cordero, Cochiti Pueblo

The sight of this white split-level house, perched on a high outcrop of rugged Camelback Mountain in Phoenix, is arresting. The shedlike construction, with its multiple pitched roofs, and the extensive use of glass play on geometry. Some of its unexpected circular windows read like giant portholes. The building eschews ornamentation, relying on its form to make a statement.

Pueblo Modern Architecture

The glass towers of the Dallas skyline are a pure expression of international style, but architects in New Mexico interpreted modern architectural form in a way that is more harmonious with the land and people of the region. The Pueblo revival of the 1920s emphasized picturesque architectural details. Even in Pueblo Deco buildings, the modern streamlined aesthetic is overwhelmed by nostalgic sentiment. So it is not surprising that New Mexican architects were among the first American architects to break away from the international style. Not forgetting the first rule of modernism that less is more, these architects allowed adobe to soar against the sky in unbroken sweeps of pure form.

Glade Sperry and Cindy Terry of Westwork Architects in Albuquerque oriented this house to the south, so its large window wall floods the room with light.

Ganado Navajo rug by Desbah Evans, Cross Canyon, Arizona

McHugh and Kidder's Santa Fe Opera, built in 1967, and Antoine Predock's La Luz condominiums in Albuquerque, built in 1968, boldly broke away from the romantic and picturesque aspects of Pueblo revival to interpret Pueblo forms in abstract, geometric compositions. Traditional exterior features, including *viga* roof projections and *portales,* are highly stylized. Both buildings introduce a dynamic relationship between construction and landscape, between outside and inside. Each building's form and its relationship to its site are more important to the design than ornament or historic reference.

This home in Albuquerque was designed by Berent Groth. It has the openness of one of Frank Lloyd Wright's designs and uses straightforward building materials and white surface treatments to manipulate light. This sitting area is set off from the dining area and atrium behind it with a floating wall.

221

The palette in this Scottsdale, Arizona, home was kept natural, from flagstone floors to neutral tones used for furnishings. The glass doors look out to the pool, backyard, and a view of the city.

Predock's reputation as New Mexico's leading architect has been achieved by his remarkable and evocative interpretation of the Southwestern landscapes and cityscapes in his buildings. Witty, unexpected references and bold forms are Predock's forte in a wide range of buildings, including a Taos "Mountain" house, an adobe "Italian hill townhouse," an Albuquerque Route 66 apartment complex of colored stucco and neon trim, and a new "Santa Fe" hotel for EuroDisneyland that borrows themes from drive-in movie theaters.

Architect Carlos Jimenez was commissioned to remodel a two-story masonry and stucco home in Houston. Radically changed, the former living room became a dining room, with a vaulted ceiling, fireplace, and central light well. An alcove echoes the width and volume of the light well. A buffet credenza was built into a portion of the alcove space. Track lighting unobtrusively illuminates the room. Furnishings are also simple; the pedestal table has been in the family for many years.

Only three colors were used throughout the interior of Ken Ronchetti's home: black, straw, and white. Ronchetti divided the home spatially and functionally into three parts: master bedroom and guest suites, entertainment area, and kitchen and dining area.

A modern interpretation of Southwest style leans on architecture for drama. To play up the traditional beamed ceiling, designer Lawrence Lake gave the plaster walls texture. Lake designed the cantilevered Corian countertop, with a nod to Frank Lloyd Wright.

Architect Ken Ronchetti was inspired by Southwest pueblos and Mayan temples when he designed this home near San Diego. Simple planes create a compelling abstract pattern. The forms catch the sun in the winter and reflect it in summer.

Architect Lawrence Speck designed a Texas-sized kitchen for this ranch in Wimberly. The kitchen, which is in the center of the house, allows simultaneous preparation of more than one meal. The living/dining area beyond the kitchen boasts a large stone fireplace and views of the Blanco River.

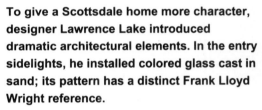

To give a Scottsdale home more character, designer Lawrence Lake introduced dramatic architectural elements. In the entry sidelights, he installed colored glass cast in sand; its pattern has a distinct Frank Lloyd Wright reference.

Pueblo modern interiors are a sculptural variation on the serene interplay of pure form and expansive space that is typical of international style at its best. In decorating strongly dramatic spaces, anything goes but nothing or very little may go better. Decorators may choose traditional Southwest furnishings of any period, but machine-age furniture, such as pieces produced by the German Bauhaus school or by American designers Charles Eames or Eliel Saarinen, are appropriate for a Pueblo modern house. Some designers maintain a modern style in all the rooms; others take an eclectic attitude, mixing and matching Southwest and modern, with spectacular results.

This fireplace wall soars nearly 18 feet. Its drama comes not only from its height but from designer Lawrence Lake's use of materials and pattern. Framed by a pair of stucco columns with reveals, the central core is tiled in concrete mixed with chips of sparkling amethyst. The dramatic neon sculpture is by Randy McCabe.

Lawrence Lake designed this entertainment unit and wedged it between two scored columns. The console is made of faux stone with an inlay of stainless steel. Above the console is a piece by Masoud Yasami, a Scottsdale artist. The area rug was made by Scott Weiland in a Wright design.

A Pool with a View

To accommodate the homeowners' request for a lap pool, architect Hugh Knoell put it in the entry and used it as a design element to highlight the architecture. During the day the sloped skylighted roof fills the space with light. At night lights from other rooms sparkle through the glass-block wall. When you walk into this house in Phoenix, you look down a series of spaces to the outside. The pool appears to continue outside the front door, with a stream of water cascading down to a pond.

This home is not so much influenced by architectural references as the nature of the site itself, says architect Hugh Knoell. The homeowners wanted to leave the desert landscape as undisturbed as possible, while they captured its drama and a magnificent view of Phoenix. Because the geometry of the house is based on the contours of the land, cantilevered roofs look like rock outcroppings. In the master bedroom, a corner window takes in the view.

A formal living room steps down to the informal family room. The house is sited on a hill, and the interior follows the steps down. The fireplace is designed so that you can see over it. Its flues are constructed of brushed stainless steel and further serve to define the open space.

Southwest Postmodern Design

As architects and their clients began to tire of the monotony of modernism, many designers turned to traditional vernacular houses for new ideas. By  the 1970s this movement away from international style was being called postmodernism. Robert Venturi developed a philosophy of postmodern architecture that championed "complexity and contradiction." Other architects had different ideas about the direction in which building design should go.

This recently redecorated 1920s stucco home in Malibu, California, is a perfect example of postmodern eclecticism in the Southwest. Designer Barbara Windum furnished the den with comfortable sofas upholstered in lush chenille. The travertine marble table, with its columnar fluted base, adds a classic touch. Its jagged irregular top suggests antiquity, an effective foil to the slick seating.

Over the last 20 years, the term postmodern has come to indicate no particular style but rather a creative reinterpretation of any and all historic design styles. Architectural elements, such as classical columns or Spanish gothic arches, are redesigned or enlarged, becoming the central motif of a postmodern building. Architectural styles are combined in new ways to create a hybrid style. Historic designs are updated and expressed with contemporary materials. The availability of recently developed industrial building components has given postmodern architects wider ranges of colors, textures, and effects than has ever before been available.

Although Santa Fe interior designer Fritz Kailer didn't alter the basic bones of the living room of his territorial stucco home, some changes made a dramatic difference. He added 14 feet of skylight and installed track lighting around its perimeter. Kailer remodeled the fireplace opening, introducing an arch to echo the entry, and fitted it with a hinged fire screen. Although he did not change the windows, he camouflaged what he feels is a weak feature by swagging cotton duck over specially designed rods. The eclectic furnishings combine Louis XVI lounge chairs with pine frames and a waterfall-armed sofa, upholstered in textured cotton.

An Acoma seed pot by Diane Lewis

This home north of El Paso, Texas, doubles as an airplane hangar. As many as three planes can be parked on the ground floor. Above is the main living level, with a bedroom on each side. There also is a spacious kitchen. Architect David E. Hilles incorporated cedar and El Paso limestone in the framework, and the floors are paved with Arizona flagstone.

Stickley chairs covered in cowhide join Arts and Crafts sensibilities with Southwest naturalism. To leave this cozy interior, all homeowner Malcolm McGregor has to do is to open the 80-foot door, rev up one of his 1930s or 1940s airplanes, and take off from his own runway.

Inspired eclecticism guides postmodern interior design. Art furniture, neoclassical and antique pieces, country furniture, and Santa Fe design are all part of the postmodern vocabulary. There are no pure styles anymore and no rules to follow. This anything-goes attitude has made Southwest style an important element of many homes in many different parts of the world. In the Southwest the postmodern reinvestigations and contemporary expressions of regional style have reopened a dialogue between old and new that began with Pueblo Deco designers. Nowhere in America does an architect or interior designer have as many historic architectural styles, construction techniques, colors, or furniture styles from which to select his or her own unique Southwest expressions.

David Hilles describes his architecture for this Texan home as "fairly prairie style but more contemporary": a good definition of this premier Southwest postmodern mode. A combination of El Paso limestone and cedar, with a cedar shingle roof, the building has the rustic charm of a lodge. The 35-foot-high space is braced with three steel trusses.

Postmodern Design

Southwest architects began to appreciate regional and local housing traditions long before historic preservation and reinterpretation caught on in the rest of the country. The successful preservationist movement in the Southwest is encouraged by an ongoing grass roots effort to survey and protect the region's wealth of historic architecture. A steady influx of people from other parts of the country to the Southwest during the past 30 years has helped to make designers everywhere aware of Southwest design themes. National interest in Southwest arts, crafts, furniture, and design creates a growing market that encourages a strengthening of the Southwest regional aesthetic.

Today anyone anywhere can become a successful Southwest designer. All you need is a working knowledge of the region's rich architectural legacy, an awareness of traditional building materials, a lively sense of color, a dash of humor, and a collector's eye for juxtaposing the contemporary with the traditional.

The stylized sun and flowers in this bowl sink, from the Kohler Artist Editions Reveries Collection, reflect both Southwest and Egyptian design motifs.

Designer Christine Geiselhart brought rustic touches to the crisp architecture of this Santa Fe adobe. A graceful wrought-iron chandelier hangs over a pine table, teamed with rush-seat chairs.

A tiled island, shaped like a waterfall, is the centerpiece in this kitchen of a Scottsdale home designed by Adolf deRoy Mark.

High tech meets Pueblo style in this kitchen designed by William Tull for a home in Carefree, Arizona.

236

California Expressions

California's classic Southwest styles, including Monterey, mission revival, and Spanish colonial revival, give designers a dynamic set of themes with which to work. But the cosmopolitan design industry in California has greatly expanded from this historic foundation to develop a myriad of possibilities. Some California designers of Southwest expressions have borrowed heavily from popular Santa Fe design styles, but they have interpreted them with glamorous, high-style overtones. Mirrors, chrome, polished brass, and neon accent natural wood and stucco in these interiors. Delighting in unique, one-of-a-kind finishes, Los Angeles designers pioneered a rustic peeling-paint effect that exposes several different colors of paint, applied to such traditional New Mexican colonial pieces as *trasteros*, tables, and *sillas*, or armchairs.

This central vaulted ceiling lends an expansiveness to the space, with the symmetrical fireplace anchoring the room's center. Along with the fireplace, the home is heated with passive solar energy; tile floors on the main level absorb heat from the sun.

The forms of this southern California stucco home are seen as abstract planes, recalling the slab walls and punched openings of California mission style. Architect Rob Wellington Quigley used two windows on the north elevation to call attention to the entrance, which has a canopy of wire glass to reduce heat loss.

239

When architect Bart Prince designed a home for his parents in Albuquerque, he wanted to make it a postmodern expression of the Southwest. The radiating skylighted ceiling of this living room recalls circular towers with Pueblo and Spanish references. Prince's forms are unique expressions, but this home definitely has a strong Southwest feeling in its use of natural materials and the relationship of the house to the earth. The grand fireplace is made from granite taken from the site. *Nichos* seem like natural indentations, with their staggered placement. The floor is silver quartz slate. There is an abundance of glass to take advantage of the views of mountains on one side and the Rio Grande valley on the other.

Textiles for upholstery, pillow covers, and curtains are imported to the West Coast from Mexico, Guatemala, and Peru, and this use of imported fabrics has become appropriate for Southwest rooms in Santa Fe and elsewhere. California designers have long been interested in the extraordinary range of fabrics, furnishings, and accessories made in Mexico and Latin America. Colonial-design mesquite furniture, colorful ceramic sculptures, and brightly painted folk-carved animals are common interior accents in California homes. Traditional Hispanic tinwork and wrought iron are used in postmodern interiors for picture frames, light fixtures, lamp shades, and light-switch plates, with images based on Anasazi petroglyph symbols.

Like a contemporary organic pueblo or kiva, an undulating wood wall envelops spiral stairs to the master bedroom in a Los Altos, California, house designed by Bart Prince.

New Mexico Expressions

The Southwest design center, Santa Fe, started to break free of the dominant Pueblo revival movement in the 1960s, as modernist architects began to exploit the primal sculptural and planar qualities of the adobe aesthetic. By the 1980s postmodern architecture had arrived in New Mexico with unexpected and delightful results. Adobe architecture was celebrated by writers, architects, and photographers; the Pompidou Centre in Paris mounted a major exhibition called "Earth Architecture" in 1981. The exhibit pointed out the crosscultural similarities of African, Islamic, and Southwest adobe architectural traditions, inspiring designers to combine elements of all three. An adobe mosque, designed by Egyptian architect Hassan Fathy, was built in Abiquiu, New Mexico, in 1981, further illustrating the international design potential of adobe. In his spectacular house and studio, artist James Jereb combined Moorish and Santa Fe architecture and interior design styles. White Moorish arches glow in contrast with walls that are colored mustard, cobalt blue, or vermilion. African art and wall hangings look at home in Jereb's desert oasis.

A painted and carved wall leads to James Jereb's courtyard. Jereb painted the walls in different shades of terra cotta and sand.

A Guatemalan mask hangs on the wall of the front porch of James Jereb's home. Firewood is stored in the corner. The basket is from Mexico. The home is about 80 years old.

Egyptian architect Hassan Fathy incorporated a starlike web design in an adobe mosque in Abiquiu, New Mexico.

Designer James Jereb embellished the traditional corner fireplace in his bedroom with snakes and Native American symbols. Moroccan tiles border the top of the window and the base of the brick hearth. A Berber saddlebag hangs on the wall, and Berber pots sit on the window sill. A bamboo chair sports a cushion covered with African fabric.

Garden Living

When designer Lynn McEvers-Mehren moved into her adobe home in Phoenix, Arizona, she knew that she would remodel the garden, in addition to changing the interior space. The house, which has a tile roof matched inside by a coffered mahogany ceiling, melds architectural styles that were in fashion when it was built in 1923.

The homeowner loves gardening, and she wanted to combine California and English garden styles in her plans. "I wanted to create a series of microenvironments," she says. To achieve the look she was after, McEvers-Mehren included a variety of unusual objects in her garden. On one side of the house, a mirror joins pieces from an old fireplace. One seating area includes cedar lodge-pole furniture and a half-round stucco bench.

The garden includes everything anyone would want for outdoor living. There is a kitchen, a fireplace to warm chilly evenings, and a spot for casual dining, as well as a wet bar. The pride of the garden is an antique bench that the homeowner found in Bath, England. A tall Italian stone fountain has three built-in bowls. The large bowl is for horses; the bowl nearest the ground is for cats and dogs, and the uppermost bowl is for people.

Texas Expressions

Many Texans have turned to Europe, New York, or California when they wanted to build or decorate their homes and offices. Such famous architects as Philip Johnson, Louis I. Kahn, and I.M. Pei have built many major commissions in Texas. This trend is not surprising given the multinational scope of many Texas-based businesses and the lack of a truly Texas architectural vernacular.

Aside from cowboy and ranch style, Texas has lacked a major residential design style to call its own. The Spanish and Mexican colonial periods were brief, and the population was too small and scattered to develop its own unique architecture. Log houses dotted the vast prairie and low hills until well into the twentieth century, when Texas's population began to expand rapidly. East Coast architecture, including Victorian frame houses, stucco bungalows, and international style ranch houses and glass office towers, has been successfully introduced in Texas.

The fir railing, says Austin architect Robert Kahler, is a direct interpretation of Santa Fe notched balusters. Two styles of brackets recall the diversity of territorial *portales.* Encasing the loftlike living space with glass instead of cedar maximized the outdoor relationship.

When architect Robert Kahler was commissioned to design an addition for an Austin, Texas, home, he brought the 1960s house up to date with a postmodern flourish. The roof of a one-story garage was removed and a master bedroom was built atop. Then the breezeway between the garage and the home was roofed over, creating a charming interior courtyard. The iron railing and spiral stairs, crafted by a local blacksmith, reinterpret Spanish colonial style.

An iron bed on a screened-in second-level porch is a favorite place for sleeping when the weather is warm. Iron chairs and a glass-topped iron table are positioned to take advantage of a lovely canyon view.

The French doors in the master bedroom lead to a sleeping porch. The cozy grouping in front of the fireplace includes a coffee table made from a cypress stump and side tables found at a garage sale. The deer-antler chandelier adds ambience.

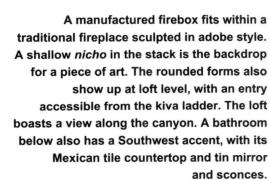

A view of the bridge in Robert Kahler's Austin ranch

A manufactured firebox fits within a traditional fireplace sculpted in adobe style. A shallow *nicho* in the stack is the backdrop for a piece of art. The rounded forms also show up at loft level, with an entry accessible from the kiva ladder. The loft boasts a view along the canyon. A bathroom below also has a Southwest accent, with its Mexican tile countertop and tin mirror and sconces.

After World War II, a large Hispanic population with strong ties to Mexico developed in the south Texas cities of San Antonio, Corpus Christi, and Brownsville. As Southwest style has become steadily more popular throughout America, Mexican and Mexican-American art and architecture have become popular in Texas. Architects have also created stunning reinterpretations of historic ranch and farm houses. They used such traditional materials as limestone, adobe, logs, and lumber, but applied modern techniques to create soaring interior volumes.

Texas interiors combine Santa Fe design, Mexican arts and crafts, ranch and cowboy collectibles, and works of emerging Texas Hispanic artists along with all kinds of modern furniture and antiques. Color is less important than texture in the Texas home. Leather, hides, wrought iron, wood, and stone are the basic building blocks of the exciting Texas homestyle.

Having It All

Designed by the architectural firm of Ford, Powell and Carson, this ranch house near Laredo, Texas, was built from native Mexican stone and topped with a standing galvanized metal roof. The stepped stone walls are consistent with regional architecture, and the deep window reveals act as light monitors. Copper poles hold handmade lanterns, which light the path to the entrance.

A screened-in porch, which wraps around the house, adds another option for enjoying the outdoors to the all-seasons pleasure of this delightful home. On a nippy day, the homeowners can bundle up and sit by a fire. When it's hot, they admire the view from inside, where air conditioning keeps them cool. When the breezes are gentle, they choose to sit on one of the porch's *equipale* chairs.

The big hearth, the focal point of the eat-in kitchen, is made of single slabs of stone from the Laredo area. The herringbone doors are patterned after old barn doors, which are typical in the vernacular architecture. The rich blue of the tile floors is complemented with a collection of blue-and-white porcelain, which hangs on the wall above the fireplace. The thickness of the walls is evident from the window recesses.

An old English oak table is teamed with a *banco* that hugs a large picture window. The *banco* and chairs, woven rattan from Old Hickory, are upholstered in Guatemalan fabric from Mimi London. Barbara Windum designed the tile for the risers, which was inspired by patterns probably manufactured in the late 1920s.

Southwest Expressions

The Spanish Southwest has a fascinating history, culture, and design tradition. Southwest design is full of romance, handcrafted beauty, and spiritual yearnings, and its recent popularity has encouraged a reinvestigation of the entire Southwest. Today a new and exciting regional style is emerging. It is based on the ancient adobe construction of the Pueblos and Spanish colonists, and the unsurpassed craftsmanship of Southwest and Latin American artists. Whether walls are painted in desert or tropical colors, Southwest style reflects a relaxed way of life.

Contemporary seating and bold colors characterize this living room in Malibu, California. The tiles surrounding the fireplace are new but pressed from old molds. The window, which has an unpromising view, is masked with hanging plants. The rug was designed by Barbara Windum and expresses a Southwest theme. The dining chairs are from Foreign Traders in Santa Fe.

An archway, dramatized in a vivid tangerine, looks into the main living room of James Jereb's Santa Fe home. The door, which opens to a front porch, is painted in a striking chevron pattern, adapted from a North African design. Portions of the top and bottom elements of the panels and the door jamb were painted blue, a New Mexican trademark that Spanish settlers believed kept out evil spirits. The antique pine table is New Mexican. Above the fireplace hangs a nineteenth-century painting of a North African.

A French poster dated 1931 hangs in the stairwell of artist James Jereb's Santa Fe adobe. Decorative glazed tiles from Morocco were set into the wall, a technique that also has Southwest roots and is often seen in Spanish colonial design.

A contemporary home in Scottsdale reflects the adobe vernacular. The projecting *vigas* create interesting shadows across the facade; squarish columns frame the enclosed porch.